# Common Southwestern
# Native Plants

# Common Southwestern Native Plants:
## An Identification Guide

Jack L. Carter
Martha A. Carter
Donna J. Stevens

Mimbres Publishing
Silver City, NM

Published by Mimbres Publishing
P. O. Box 1244
Silver City, New Mexico, 88062


Common Southwestern Native Plants: An Identification Guide
Jack L. Carter, Martha A. Carter and Donna J. Stevens

ISBN 0-9619945-1-7

Library of Congress Control Number: 2003095105


Printed by Johnson Printing
Distributed by Johnson Books
1880 South 57th Court, Boulder, Colorado 80301
1-800-258-5830
E-mail: books©jpcolorado.com


Cover: Howellgraphics.com
Silver City, NM
Cover photo: Ralph A. Fisher, Jr.

# CONTENTS

# INTRODUCTION

"The earth's vegetation is part of the web of life in which there are intimate and essential relationships between plants and the earth, between plants and other plants, between plants and animals. Sometimes we have no choice but to disturb these relationships, but we should do so thoughtfully, with full awareness that what we do may have consequences remote in time and place."
Rachel Carson (1907-1964) *Silent Spring*. 1962

For many people, learning about plants and the natural world is a new experience and is not easy. To people who have lived their lives in large metropolitan areas, as most of us commonly do today, the idea of moving into a new and different environment can be frightening. Learning to critically observe, enjoy and be a part of nature requires a different kind of thinking and lifestyle.

For some time the only plants many people have been seriously interested in were those that went into a salad, or house plants they might pick up on a K-Mart or Wal-Mart "blue light" special to bring a little beauty into their homes. Grandparents knew about flower gardens, picking wild berries for jellies, canning fresh vegetables from the garden, and yards with giant shade trees. But the young have long considered their grandparents' lives to be rather boring.

Between World War I and World War II, the U.S. rapidly shifted from a rural, agricultural and gardening nation to a nation of city dwellers. We literally worked very hard to escape our roots in favor of city life, with speedy cars, air conditioning and fast foods. Our predominant travel is from city to city, either flying or racing down a four lane highway to the next rest area. We would rather not be bothered by the flora and fauna, because we have not considered such living things as part of our environment. If we ventured outside it was for a walk on a manicured golf course or park, or to visit a zoo where all the animals were safely behind bars. Today society demands that even our baseball and football stadiums be enclosed so that our total environment can be completely controlled and separate from the natural world.

However, change is in the breezes. Those of us who have devoted many years to urging the conservation of the natural world and to the study of natural history can now report that, for a variety of reasons, "conservation" is

1

again a good word. In the past 10 or 15 years we have observed some shifts in the way more and more people see their world. They seem to be recognizing that there is more to life than moving from place to place as rapidly as possible. Reducing our speed so that we may smell the flowers is attracting the interest of many more people today.

Greater numbers of people are recognizing they must learn more about the local and regional flora if they are going to make sound decisions concerning the conservation of the natural world, including humankind. Today ever larger groups of people with limited knowledge of the flora and fauna, are asking a wide range of questions. On field trips we hear over and over such statements as: What is the name of that plant? This is a beautiful tree! Is it a native species or an introduced species? Would that shrub grow in my yard? Would it be OK for me to collect some seeds? Newcomers to the Southwest are extremely eager to learn, and are full of important questions. And many people of all ages, who have lived their lives in this region, are becoming aware of the connections between the limited available water in the area, the climate, and the native flora that has survived untold droughts and still flourishes.

In recent years memberships are growing in organizations devoted to gardening with native plants, taking field trips to natural areas, and conducting short courses to learn more about the local flora, soils and water. Many individuals are recognizing that the green that once resided only in their thumbs is rapidly spreading throughout their bodies, and becoming a part of all their senses. State highway departments find that people are extremely interested in roadside plantings, weed control and highway beautification, even to the point where clubs and civic organizations will help maintain roadsides. Private landscapers and nurseries are being called on by increasing numbers of people to provide and plant native species.

What appears to be unfolding within the senses of literally huge numbers of people is the realization that nature and our environment form an extremely complex dynamic of millions of bits and pieces. Green plants, through photosynthesis, form the foundation of all life. Both the living and nonliving systems, working together through evolution, have provided us with all we have at our disposal. We are recognizing that Garrett Hardin was exactly correct when he encouraged us to keep in mind that when dealing with the natural world, we can never do just <u>one</u> thing. The green mantle that covers the earth is our home and we should be extremely careful when disturbing it. We must always keep in mind that the term, "ecology" comes from the Greek word *Oikos*, which means home. The Earth is our only home.

This publication is an extension of the belief systems of those who brought it to reality. We believe that no person can live a full and fruitful life without understanding the place of plants in the past, present, and future of all animals, including humankind.

## ABOUT THIS BOOK

"He is happiest who hath the power to gather wisdom from a flower."

Mary Howitt, 1799-1888, British Poet

This book is for all those folks who enjoy walking a trail in one of our state or national forests or other natural areas throughout the Southwest. We have brought together a pictorial guide that will assist those with a limited knowledge of the flora to recognize some of the trees overhead and some of the shrubs and herbaceous plants along the trail. It is for people who want to get to know more about some common native plant species that form the beautiful backdrop we describe as enchanting. It will provide a starting point for learning some common native plant species so beginners can walk into a nursery and ask to see some native plants by name, plants they know are appropriate for their lawn or garden.

We like to think this is not a scientific book, but a publication for those who are just starting to inquire about the plants right where they live, or as they travel, in the Southwest. Although this book includes both scientific and common names, it also features plant descriptions, illustrations and attractive color photographs, and could be defined as a botanical field primer. It is designed for people who are just beginning to explore, and want to place a name on, the trees, shrubs or herbs in their immediate environment. We have intentionally included 145 of the most common native plants encountered while hiking in a national forest or state park throughout the southwestern United States. Experience has taught us that field guides of 400 or 500 species are great for those with a background in field botany, but intimidating for beginning students.

Experience also tells us that most beginners are numbed and confused when we try to lay more than 10 or 15 new plant names on them during a single field outing. We, along with most botanists, talk too much. When students ask for the name of a plant, the common name is usually all they want to know at that time. But we teachers feel compelled to push the scientific name, family name, and all the additional information we have in our bag of pent up knowledge. Students are actually well qualified to ask additional questions for which they want answers, and will ask for the scientific and family names when they are ready.

An additional word about plant names in this book -- as you identify a plant, you will find a common name, or several common names, in bold type, and this may be all you wish to know. For those who are interested, the common name(s) will be followed by the single best scientific name, and this is followed by the plant family to which this species belongs. The scientific name is made up of a binomial, or two names: the generic name (genus) and the specific name (specific epithet). These two terms form the scientific name of that particular plant species and are always in italics. You will also find we have added some synonyms following the correct scientific name. These are names that were at one time the scientific name in use for this species, but for any of several reasons, have been changed to a new name or have reverted back to a previous one. We have added some of the common synonyms in this publication for those folks who may have originally studied a plant under a previous scientific name and recognize it by that earlier name.

The three individuals listed on the front of this book have worked closely for the past three years to bring it to completion. We want it to work as a guide for beginning students rather than as a complete flora of all the plants of the Southwest. Most laypersons will be able to pick up the book for the first time, and by thumbing through the several basic sections, see a number of trees, shrubs and herbaceous plants that they recognize and for which they would like to learn more.

We feel certain the colored plates will attract the readers to the beauty of our native flora and provide a greater appreciation for the soft colors that define the Southwest. With the colored plates, illustrations and short descriptions, we have included an expanded view of each of these common plant species. The last 13 pages of the colored photographs (pages 62 to 74) feature 38 common herbaceous flowering plants with short descriptions of each. These plants are widely spread over the landscape and along roadsides, and are commonly planted in our gardens. Our wish is that these plants will become an important part of the plant vocabulary of far greater numbers of people.

The terminology has been kept to a minimum and the reading material provides some common, but also some not so common, historical information about these species. If you are interested in a very short course in field botany, please take a trip through the glossary and the illustrated glossary. We must warn you that the only way to use this information is with a plant specimen in hand. The terms and illustrations in the glossary are not to be studied, and certainly not memorized, but should be learned in the field while observing living plants. Experience tells us that cacti are much better recognized when we feel them than when we read about them!

All of the plants included were growing in the Southwest long before our species ever migrated to the region; thus their history has an extremely important story to tell. For this reason you will note that we have included the term "native" in the title. Two definitions about which there is considerable confusion in many people's minds may be helpful. Native or indigenous species are those that have evolved over millions of years in a floristic region, life zone or ecosystem and are naturally dispersed within that area. They have been subjected to long periods of natural selection and their presence aids us in describing the Southwest. At the same time, introduced species evolved naturally in Asia, Europe, Africa, the Middle East or elsewhere and have been transported chiefly by *Homo sapiens* from one region to another. These species we usually refer to as aliens or exotics. Some common troublesome introduced species include Russian Olive, *Elaeagnus angustifolia*; Salt Cedar, *Tamarix chinensis*; Siberian Elm, *Ulmus pumila*; Tree of Heaven, *Ailanthus altissima*; Bindweed, *Convolvulus arvensis*; and Purple Loosestrife, *Lythrum salicaria*.

The **References and Suggested Readings** list on pages 206 and 207 will allow those students seeking additional information to extend their knowledge of the included species. We have listed a number of publications that will allow individuals to develop a much deeper knowledge of the multitude of relationships among plants and people.

On a personal note, this book might be considered as a thank you message to the hundreds of students and friends who have joined us on camping and field trips into the Southwest over the past 40 years. Field botany classes from Colorado College in Colorado Springs traveled the Southwest for several weeks at a time, raising endless questions concerning the flora. We also wish to recognize Elderhostel groups, scout troops and service club members who bring so much enthusiasm to the learning process. And above all, we wish to thank Native Plant Society members who are committed to knowing and protecting the native flora.

As part of the learning process we have continuously visited new places throughout the Southwest and stopped to study the flora that surrounded us. The San Juan National Forest, Canyon de Chelly National Monument, Salt River Canyon, the Southwest Research Station, Chiricahua National Monument, the Coronado and Gila National Forests all provided opportunities to camp and study. There were also field excursions to the Great Sand Dunes National Monument, Fort Union National Monument, Santa Fe National Forest, Bandelier National Monument, Guadalupe Mountains National Park, and the Davis Mountains. These landmarks and many others literally describe the geographic range of this book. When you are traveling through the great Southwest, you will want to make every effort to visit these very special places.

# ACKNOWLEDGMENTS

Martha Carter has been the driving force behind this book. It has been her enthusiasm, first to learn more about the flora of the southwest and second, her interest in plant photography, computers and layout that has led to the completion of this book. Martha is worthy of the title artist, botanist, layout specialist and editor. She has a work ethic that is embarrassing for the rest of us, and she knows how to make things happen.

Donna Stevens has become an integral part of the Carters' professional activities over the past six years. Joining them while still an undergraduate at Western New Mexico University, they soon recognized her intellectual enthusiasm and her skills in the use of the English language. Over this period of time, she has grown to become an outstanding field botanist and herbarium curator. And above all this, she is a joy to work with. It was only natural for Donna to become an important part of this publication.

Jack Carter has been an enthusiastic student of the natural world for more than half a century. During this time, his many years of teaching have taught him that there is a giant gap between science and society. His career and publications center on the place of knowledge in the development of human values. This book is for him just one more attempt to bring plants and people closer together, so they might both survive in a world of limits.

The illustrations in this publication are primarily the work of three talented artists. Beth Dennis, Marjorie C. Leggitt, and William Underwood made these drawings for our earlier book titled *Trees and Shrubs of New Mexico*. As we study the detail in the quality of their outstanding line drawings, we recognize the importance of good illustrations in floristic work. Also included are illustrations by Harry Stover, Marilyn Huggins and Susan Rubin.

Dr. Richard Johnson, Professor of Math and Computer Sciences, Western New Mexico University, provided technical assistance with desktop publishing. Laura Howell, Howell Graphic Design, Silver City, assisted with art and graphic layout and provided encouragement and support. We would especially like to thank Robert Sivinski for bringing his scientific expertise and editorial skills to this publication.

Ralph Fisher had an important role to play in planning this book. Ralph became a very close friend when, soon after we moved to Silver City, we met him through the Gila Chapter of the Native Plant Society of New Mexico and the Southwest Audubon Chapter. He was the perfect example of an educated layperson, with extreme interest in the natural history of the Southwest. Alone or with a friend, he continuously traveled throughout the region in search of that plant or animal he had not previously encountered, and would not let up until he had a name for that species. He enjoyed collecting plants and was an avid photographer. Once or twice each week during the growing season he would pull into our yard with a plant or some slides that required identification. Some years ago we encouraged Ralph to publish a book in which he could use his many excellent slides, but he always said that wasn't something he would tackle. Wanting to see his slides used for education, he was always generous in giving us slides for our collection, knowing that someday they would go to the Native Plant Society of New Mexico. Ralph died in 2000. He was a dear friend and we still miss having him drop by for a visit. He would be pleased to know that a number of his photographs appear in this book.

In addition to the photographs of Ralph Fisher and Jack and Martha Carter, we must credit former Colorado College students, and Andy Wasowski and Ron Gibbs of the Native Plant Society of New Mexico for completing the collection chosen for this publication.

May this small book assist you in becoming not only more knowledgeable of the plants that surround you, but aid you in developing a better understanding of the connections between plants and people.

Jack L. Carter
22 July 2003

# Organization of the Photographs

# GYMNOSPERMS - CONE BEARING PLANTS

**ARIZONA CYPRESS,
CEDRO**
*Cupressus arizonica*
Page 76

seed cones

**COMMON JUNIPER,
DWARF JUNIPER**
*Juniperus communis*
Page 77

seed cones

seed cones

bark

**ALLIGATOR JUNIPER**
*Juniperus deppeana*
Page 78

seed cones

**ONE-SEEDED JUNIPER**
*Juniperus monosperma*
Page 79

**ROCKY MOUNTAIN
JUNIPER**
*Juniperus scopulorum*
Page 80

seed cones

**WHITE FIR,
BALSAM FIR**
*Abies concolor*
Page 81

seed cones

gall

**COLORADO BLUE SPRUCE,
SILVER SPRUCE**
*Picea pungens*
Page 82

**COLORADO BRISTLECONE PINE,
FOXTAIL PINE**
*Pinus aristata*
(showing *krummholz*
effect at high elevations)
Page 83

seed cone

pollen cones

**PINYON PINE** **15**
*Pinus edulis*
Page 84

seed cone

**LIMBER PINE**
*Pinus flexilis*
Page 85 - 86

**SOUTHWESTERN WHITE PINE**
*Pinus strobiformis*
seed cones
Page 85 - 86

16

seed cones

**PONDEROSA PINE,
WESTERN YELLOW PINE**
*Pinus ponderosa*
Page 87

**DOUGLAS FIR**
*Pseudotsuga menziesii*
Page 88

seed cone

pollen-bearing strobili

seed-bearing strobili

**MORMON TEA, BIG JOINT FIR,
TORREY JOINT FIR**
*Ephedra trifurca*
Page 89

# TREES

**ARIZONA WALNUT,
NOGAL SILVESTRE**
*Juglans major*
Page 94

**BOX ELDER,
FRESNO DE GUAJUCO**
*Acer negundo*
Page 93

18

**VELVET ASH,
ARIZONA ASH**
*Fraxinus velutina*
Page 95

**ARIZONA SYCAMORE,
ARIZONA PLANE-TREE**
*Platanus wrightii*
Page 96

**NARROWLEAF COTTONWOOD**
*Populus angustifolia*
Page 97

**COTTONWOODS: FREMONT, ALAMO** and **PLAINS**
*Populus deltoides*
Page 98

**LANCELEAF COTTONWOOD,
SMOOTH-BARKED COTTONWOOD**
*Populus* X *acuminata*
Page 99

staminate catkins

**GOODDING'S WILLOW,
WESTERN BLACK WILLOW**
*Salix gooddingii*
Page 100

**WESTERN SOAPBERRY, JABONCILLO**
*Sapindus saponaria*
Page 101

# SMALL TREES OR SHRUBS

**ROCKY MOUNTAIN MAPLE**
*Acer glabrum*
Page 103

**BIGTOOTH MAPLE**
*Acer grandidentatum*
Page 104

female catkins            male catkins

**THINLEAF ALDER,**
**MOUNTAIN ALDER**
*Alnus incana* ssp. *tenuifolia*
Page 105

**DESERT WILLOW, MIMBRE**
*Chilopsis linearis*
Page 106

**NEW MEXICO ELDER,
BLUEBERRY ELDER**
*Sambucus cerulea*
Page 107

**ROCKY MOUNTAIN ELDER**
*Sambucus racemosa* var. *microbotrys*
Page 108

**TEXAS MADRONE,
MADROÑO**
*Arbutus xalapensis*
Page 109

**NEW MEXICO LOCUST**
*Robinia neomexicana*
Page 110

**GAMBEL OAK**
*Quercus gambelii*
Page 112

**EMORY OAK**
*Quercus emoryi*
Page 111

**GRAY OAK,
SCRUB OAK**
*Quercus grisea*
Page 113

**28**

**LITTLE WALNUT**
*Juglans microcarpa*
Page 114

**WESTERN CHOKECHERRY,**
**COMMON CHOKECHERRY**
*Prunus virginiana*
Page 115

**SOUTHWESTERN**
**CHOKECHERRY**
*Prunus serotina*
Page 115

**HOP TREE, WAFER ASH**
*Ptelea trifoliata*
Page 116

**QUAKING ASPEN**
*Populus tremuloides*
Page 117

30

**NETLEAF HACKBERRY,
PALO BLANCO**
*Celtis reticulata*
Page 118

bark

# SHRUBS

**DESERT HONEYSUCKLE, CHUPAROSA**
*Anisacanthus thurberi*
Page 120

**SKUNKBUSH,**
**THREE LEAF SUMAC**
*Rhus trilobata*
Page 121

**SMOOTH SUMAC,**
**SCARLET SUMAC**
*Rhus glabra*
Page 122

**SEEPWILLOW BACCHARIS**
*Baccharis salicifolia*
Page 125

**BIG SAGEBRUSH**
*Artemisia tridentata*
Page 124

**PASTURE SAGE, ESTAFIATA**
*Artemisia frigida*
Page 123

**BRICKELLBUSH,
TASSELFLOWER**
*Brickellia grandiflora*
Page 126

**TURPENTINE BUSH**
*Ericameria laricifolia*
Page 127

**RABBITBRUSH, CHAMISA**
*Ericameria nauseosa*
Page 128

**DOUGLAS GROUNDSEL**
*Senecio flaccidus* var. *douglasii*
Page 129

36

**ALGERITA, RED OREGON-GRAPE**
*Berberis haematocarpa*
Page 130

**CREEPING OREGON-GRAPE**
*Berberis repens*
Page 131

**MOUNTAIN SNOWBERRY,
ROUNDLEAF SNOWBERRY**
*Symphoricarpos rotundifolius*
Page 132

**FOUR-WINGED SALTBUSH**
*Atriplex canescens*
Page 133

**38**

**WINTERFAT,
WHITE SAGE**
*Krascheninnikovia lanata*
Page 134

**RED-OSIER DOGWOOD**
*Cornus sericea*
Page 135

**KINNIKINNICK**
*Arctostaphylos uva-ursi*
Page 137

**MANZANITA,
POINT-LEAF MANZANITA**
*Arctostaphylos pungens*
Page 136

**INDIGO BUSH, FALSE INDIGO**
*Amorpha fruticosa*
Page 138

**40**

**FAIRY DUSTER,
MESQUITILLA**
*Calliandra eriophylla*
Page 139

**FEATHER INDIGOBUSH**
*Dalea formosa*
Page 140

**BROOM DALEA**
*Psorothamnus scoparius*
Page 142

**MESQUITE,
HONEY MESQUITE**
*Prosopis glandulosa*
Page 141

**TEXAS MOUNTAIN LAUREL,
MESCAL-BEAN SOPHORA**
*Sophora secundiflora*
Page 143

42

**SILVERLEAF OAK,
WHITELEAF OAK**
*Quercus hypoleucoides*
Page 144

**OCOTILLO**
*Fouquieria splendens*
Page 145

**GOLDEN CURRANT**
*Ribes aureum*
Page 146

**WOLF'S CURRANT**
*Ribes wolfii*
Page 149

**WAX CURRANT**
*Ribes cereum*
Page 147

**ORANGE GOOSEBERRY**
*Ribes pinetorum*
Page 148

44

**CLIFF FENDLERBUSH**
*Fendlera rupicola*
Page 150

**WAXFLOWER**
*Jamesia americana*
Page 151

45

**BLUE SAGE,
SHRUBBY SALVIA**
*Salvia pinguifolia*
Page 152

**NEW MEXICO OLIVE,
NEW MEXICO FORESTIERA**
*Forestiera pubescens*
Page 153

**BUCKBRUSH,
FENDLER CEANOTHUS**
*Ceanothus fendleri*
Page 154

**DESERT CEANOTHUS,
DESERT BUCKTHORN**
*Ceanothus greggii*
Page 155

**SHADBUSH,**
**CLUSTER SERVICEBERRY**
*Amelanchier pumila*
Page 157

**BIRCH-LEAF BUCKTHORN, COFFEEBERRY**
*Frangula betulifolia*
Page 156

48

**MOUNTAIN MAHOGANY**
*Cercocarpus montanus*
Page 158

**APACHE PLUME**
*Fallugia paradoxa*
Page 159

**49**

**ROCK SPIRAEA, OCEAN SPRAY**
*Holodiscus dumosus*
Page 160

**SHRUBBY CINQUEFOIL**
*Pentaphylloides floribunda*
Page 161

50

**CLIFFROSE**
*Purshia stansburiana*
Page 163

**MOUNTAIN NINEBARK**
*Physocarpus monogynus*
Page 162

**WOOD'S ROSE**
*Rosa woodsii*
Page 164

**THIMBLE RASPBERRY,
THIMBLEBERRY**
*Rubus parviflorus*
Page 165

staminate catkins

pistillate catkins

**COYOTE WILLOW,**
**SANDBAR WILLOW**
*Salix exigua*
Page 166

staminate catkins

**BLUESTEM WILLOW**
*Salix irrorata*
Page 167

pistillate catkins

**53**

**SAND PENSTEMON**
*Penstemon ambiguus*
Page 168

**PALE WOLFBERRY,
TOMATILLO**
*Lycium pallidum*
Page 169

**CREOSOTE BUSH,
HEDIONDILLA**
*Larrea tridentata*
Page 170

# WOODY VINES

**WESTERN WHITE HONEYSUCKLE**
*Lonicera albiflora*
Page 172

**ARIZONA HONEYSUCKLE**
*Lonicera arizonica*
Page 173

**ROCKY MOUNTAIN CLEMATIS**
*Clematis columbiana*
Page 174

**55**

**WESTERN VIRGIN'S BOWER**
*Clematis ligusticifolia*
Page 176

**CANYON GRAPE**
*Vitis arizonica*
Page 178

**THICKET CREEPER**
*Parthenocissus vitacea*
Page 177

# ARBORESCENT CACTI

**ENGELMANN PRICKLY PEAR**
*Opuntia engelmannii*
Page 180

**COW'S TONGUE PRICKLY PEAR,**
**TEXAS PRICKLY PEAR**
*Opuntia engelmannii*
var. *lindheimeri*
Page 181

**PURPLE-FRUITED**
**PRICKLY PEAR**
*Opuntia phaeacantha*
Page 182

**CANDELABRA CHOLLA**
*Opuntia imbricata*
Page 183

**CANE CHOLLA**
*Opuntia spinosior*
Page 183

**PENCIL CHOLLA, DESERT CHRISTMAS CHOLLA**
*Opuntia leptocaulis*
Page 184

# AGAVE AND THEIR ALLIES

**PARRY AGAVE**
*Agave parryi*
Page 186

**WHEELER SOTOL, DESERT SPOON**
*Dasylirion wheeleri*
Page 187

**BEARGRASS, SACAHUISTA**
*Nolina microcarpa*
Page 188

**BANANA YUCCA, DATIL YUCCA**
*Yucca baccata*
Page 189-190

**SOAPTREE, PALMILLA**
*Yucca elata*
Page 190 -192

**GREAT PLAINS YUCCA**
*Yucca glauca*
Page 190-191

# HERBACEOUS PLANTS

Herbaceous plants are vascular plants that do not develop woody tissue. They nornally die back to the ground level each year regardless of their life span--annual, biennial or perennial. In our forests they form the understory, with large trees providing the canopy and shrubs, small trees, and woody vines the middle story. As we travel our highways and hear some say, "The wildflowers on the roadsides are extremely beautiful," they are normally referring to low growing herbaceous plants. This is true of the herbaceous plants pictured in this book and they are some of the showiest members of the plant communities in the Southwest. The term "wildflowers" is usually restricted to native plants growing without cultivation. However, many of these plants will do well under cultivation if we will but take the time to work with them.

### BUTTERFLY WEED
*Asclepias tuberosa*
Milkweed Family (Asclepiadaceae)

Butterfly Weed is a perfect common name for this plant. If you want to attract butterflies, you really need this species. Growing up to 3 feet tall, this beautiful milkweed has bright orange flowers in clusters up to 3 inches wide, and dark green foliage. Even its fruits are interesting: the long pods burst open, releasing silky seeds that are dispersed by the wind. Butterfly Weed is the only milkweed that doesn't have "milk" in its stems. Milkweed flowers are arranged such that insect visitors can't get away without carrying some pollen, which they then deposit on the next milkweed flower they visit.

Perennial
Dry, open grasslands & forest openings
Flowers May to September
4000 to 8000 ft.

### DESERT MARIGOLD
*Baileya multiradiata*
Sunflower Family (Asteraceae)

Desert Marigold is always a welcome sight. Its sunny yellow flowers have layers of toothed ray flowers surrounding the equally bright disk flowers in the center. The flower heads are large and conspicuous, growing well above the leaves. The stems and leaves are covered with white, woolly hairs which help to minimize water loss. This prolific bloomer is quite drought tolerant.

Annual, biennial or perennial
Dry mesas, plains, roadsides
Flowers March to October
3500 to 6500 ft.

## CHOCOLATE FLOWER
*Berlandiera lyrata*
Sunflower Family (Asteraceae)

Chocolate Flower, although a member of the very large Sunflower Family, is easy to identify. It has yellow ray flowers with maroon veins on their undersides, surrounding maroon disk flowers. When the ray flowers fall off, the remaining circular, green bracts give this plant another of its common names, "Green Eyes." Its grayish-green, velvety leaves are at ground level, so the flowers really stand out. Chocolate Flower has a distinctive chocolate aroma, especially early in the morning.

Perennial
Dry plains and hills
Flowers April to October
4000 to 7000 ft.

## BRITTLEBUSH
*Encelia farinosa*
Sunflower Family (Asteraceae)

Brittlebush is one of the earliest, perennial bloomers at very low elevations. It has bright yellow ray and disk flowers, growing on tall brittle stems, that may become woody with age, and form a rounded canopy above the leaves. *Encelia* can grow up to three feet tall. The leaves are covered with white hairs that help the plant to retain water, making it perfectly suited for hot, dry climates. The resin in the stems was chewed as gum by Native Americans, and burned for incense in early missions.

Shrubby perennial
Dry, rocky slopes
Flowers November to May
Below 3000 ft.

## BLANKET FLOWER
*Gaillardia pulchella*
Sunflower Family (Asteraceae)

You won't confuse Blanket Flower with any other members of the Sunflower Family. It's quite large, with reddish-purple ray flowers. The tips of the rays are bright yellow and deeply 3-cleft. The maroon disk flowers form a dome in the center. The lower leaves are often lobed, while the upper leaves are oblong to lanceolate. Because Blanket Flower tolerates heat and drought, it is sometimes planted along roadsides.

Annual
Open plains and hills, ponderosa forests and piñon-juniper woodlands
Flowers all summer long
3500 to 6500 ft.

### DESERT-CHICORY
*Rafinesquia neomexicana*
Sunflower Family (Asteraceae)

Although Desert-Chicory is no weed, it's in the same tribe as Dandelion, and it's easy to see the resemblance. Both have ray flowers only - no disk flowers. Desert-Chicory has fringed, white rays with purple veins on the undersides. The flower heads are up to 1.5 inches wide. *Rafinesquia* is named for Constantine Rafinesque, a botanist and reported eccentric. Desert-Chicory often grows in the shade of another plant.

Annual
Deserts and grasslands
Blooms February to May
3500 to 5500 ft.

### MEXICAN HAT
*Ratibida columnifera*
Sunflower Family (Asteraceae)

Mexican Hat is very distinctive and highly variable. Its ray flowers droop gracefully, and may be solid yellow or yellow and maroon. The maroon disk flowers form a tall column, hence the specific name *columnifera*. Native Americans used the leaves and aromatic flower heads as a tea substitute. Mexican Hat is heavily utilized by butterflies.

Perennial
Roadsides, fields, forest clearings
Blooms all summer long
5000 to 8500 ft.

### WESTERN WALLFLOWER
*Erysimum capitatum*
Mustard Family (Brassicaceae)

Western Wallflower has four petals in the shape of a cross, an arrangement typical of the mustard family. The fragrant flowers are sunny yellow in lower elevations, and deep, coppery orange higher in the mountains. It can grow up to 3 feet tall, and does well in rocky soil. Its erect, slender seed pods can be 4 inches long. At high elevations, bighorn sheep and elk graze the leaves and stems.

Biennial or perennial
Open slopes
Flowers spring through fall
5000 to 11,500 ft.

## BLADDERPOD MUSTARD
*Physaria gordonii*
Mustard Family (Brassicaceae)

In early spring, Bladderpod Mustard often carpets the desert. It may be only a few inches tall, but it's quite noticeable with four bright yellow petals and silvery green leaves. The copious hairs on the stems and leaves keep Bladderpod from drying out in arid climates. When stepped on, the bladder-like pods make a popping sound.

Annual
Deserts and dry plains
Flowers February to May
3500 to 7500 ft.

## CLARET CUP CACTUS
*Echinocereus triglochidiatus*
Cactus Family (Cactaceae)

Such fierce-looking plants, with flowers that look so delicate! The stunning scarlet petals and sepals contrast with the bright green stigma in the center. The flowers stay open for several days, so you have plenty of time to enjoy their beauty. This hedgehog cactus has cylindrical stems with parallel ribs, and grows in clumps to 12 inches tall. The genus *Echinocereus* consists of several species and many varieties within species. As evidenced by its wide elevational range, it has evolved into a wide range of habitats.

Perennial
Open hillsides and rocky ledges
Blooms March to June
4000 to 9000 ft.

## CARDINAL FLOWER
*Lobelia cardinalis*
Bluebell or Bellflower Family (Campanulaceae)

The Cardinal Flower is well named. Its flowers truly are cardinal red, with an unusual, tubular, 2-lipped shape. It has dark green, alternate, toothed leaves, and grows to 5 feet tall. *Lobelia cardinalis* attracts hummingbirds and sulphur butterflies. The genus *Lobelia* is widely distributed in the West, with but a few species. Its range extends as far south as Panama.

Perennial
Wet areas and stream banks
Flowers June to October
3000 to 7000 ft.

## MEXICAN SILENE,
## MEXICAN CATCH-FLY
*Silene laciniata*
Pink Family (Caryophyllaceae)

Mexican Silene is in the same family as the carnation, and has the same "pinked" petals. The flowers are deep red with each of the five petals deeply cleft into four divisions. The stems are sticky enough to "catch a fly." There are several species of *Silene* in the Southwest, and this one is the showiest. The sticky texture of the plants in this genus gave rise to its name, an allusion to the Greek god Silenus, who was thought to be covered with foam.

Perennial
Coniferous forests
Flowers from May to October
5500 to 10,000 ft.

### NEW MEXICO LUPINE
*Lupinus neomexicanus*
Legume Family (Fabaceae)

All southwestern lupines have palmately compound leaves, which help with their identification. They have pea-like flowers typical of the legume family. Most of our lupines are showy as well, and this one is no exception. This is an important plant for nectaring butterflies. In Texas, lupines are called Blue-bonnets, and a couple of species are identified as the state flower.

Perennial
Open woods
Blooms May to September
7000 to 8000 ft.

### BLUE SCORPIONWEED
*Phacelia* sp.
Waterleaf Family (Hydrophyllaceae)

These pretty, bluish-purple, bell-shaped flowers have colorful stamens protruding beyond the petals. The flowers are arranged in coils which resemble a scorpion's tail and earn them a common name. *Phacelias* have nectar at the base of the corolla, protected by little flaps at the bottom of the stamens. A bee has to struggle to reach the nectar, and in doing so, jars the pollen-bearing anthers. Bees then spread this pollen to the next Scorpionweed they visit.

Most *Phacelias* are annuals
Blooms in early spring
Dry soils on mesas & foothills
4000 to 5000 ft.

## GIANT-HYSSOP
*Agastache pallidiflora*
Mint Family (Lamiaceae)

Giant-Hyssop belongs to the mint family, and has the square stems, opposite leaves, and aromatic foliage characteristic of mints. The flowers are lavender and two-lipped, with four projecting stamens. All of the flowers grow at the top of stems that may reach three feet tall. *Agastache,* a widely scattered genus in North America, appears to be centered in the Southwest.

Perennial
Cliffs and moist soil in coniferous forests
Flowers July to October
7000 to 10,000 ft.

## BERGAMOT, BEE-BALM
*Monarda fistulosa* var. *menthaefolia*
Mint Family (Lamiaceae)

Bergamot is unusual, with tubular, rose pink flowers arranged in a round cluster at the tip of the stem. *Menthaefolia* means mint-leaved; the leaves can be used for tea, and for flavoring in cooking. The genus *Monarda* has historically been used medicinally. Bergamot has many common names: Lemon Mint, Horsemint, Bee-balm. This is a good plant for attracting bees, butterflies, and hummingbirds.

Perennial
Open or wooded slopes
Flowers July to October
5000 to 9000 ft.

## DESERT GLOBEMALLOW
*Sphaeralcea ambigua*
Mallow Family (Malvaceae)

Globemallows are among the easiest wildflowers to identify, even for beginners. They have bright orange (sometimes pinkish or red), five-petaled flowers with a column of yellow stamens surrounding the style in the center. This species of Globemallow, *Sphaeralcea ambigua*, is the most drought tolerant of them all. You may notice a resemblance between Globemallows and hollyhocks, which are also in the mallow family, along with cotton and okra.

Perennial
Roadsides, sandy washes, dry rocky slopes
Blooms almost year-round
Below 3500 ft.

## 68
## COLORADO FOUR O'CLOCK
*Mirabilis multiflora*
Four O'Clock Family (Nyctaginaceae)

The Four O'Clock family gets its name from its flowers which open in the late afternoon, and close in the morning. For this reason, Colorado Four O'Clock makes an excellent night garden plant. The numerous, magenta, funnel-shaped flowers grow in a rounded mound that is almost shrub-like. *Mirabilis* means "marvelous," a perfect name for this plant. The Navajo use this plant for dyes and medicines. Their name for the plant translates as "falling-on-rock," apparently because it sometimes grows at the base of boulders.

Perennial
Roadsides, sandy areas, mesas
Flowers June to August
4000 to 7500 ft.

## HARTWEG EVENING PRIMROSE
*Calylophus hartwegii*
Evening Primrose Family (Onagraceae)

These beautiful, delicate yellow flowers even look good when they're not open. The large buds are reddish with green stripes, and when the flowers wilt, they fade to pinkish orange. Like other evening primroses, these flowers open in the afternoon and evening. They are pollinated by hawk moths and hummingbirds. Most species of evening primrose produce long seed capsules on a short stem; this feature helps in field identification.

Perennial
Roadsides, hillsides, plains
Blooms April to September
3000 to 7000 ft.

## HUMMINGBIRD TRUMPET
*Epilobium canum*
Evening Primrose Family (Onagraceae)

This plant is a must for your hummingbird garden. Hummers see red, and this plant is RED, from the four tubular, crinkly, notched petals, to the protruding stamens and style. Even the seed capsules and upper leaves are somewhat reddish. The generic name comes from the Greek *epi* meaning "upon" and *lobon* meaning "capsule." The Evening Primrose family is notable for the beauty of its flowers, as exemplified by Hummingbird Trumpet.

Perennial
Canyons, washes, dry slopes
Flowers June to October
4500 to 7000 ft.

## STEMLESS EVENING PRIMROSE
*Oenothera caespitosa*
Evening Primrose Family (Onagraceae)

Stemless Evening Primrose is conspicuous for a few reasons: it blooms in early spring, even during dry years, its big flowers grow close to the ground, and, of course, its beauty. Four large, white petals surround the yellow stamens and style. The flowers open in the cool of the evening. When it's hot, the petals close up and fade to pink.

Perennial
Forest clearings, roadsides, dry slopes
Blooms April to September
4000 to 8000 ft.

## MEXICAN POPPY
*Eschscholzia californica* ssp. *mexicana*
Poppy Family (Papaveraceae)

When you notice golden desert hillsides in early spring, you're seeing Mexican Poppies. Their petals - orange to yellow to gold - form a cup that remains open in full sunlight. The bluish-green leaves are deeply divided, resembling fern fronds. The long, slender capsules contain many seeds. This genus is named for Dr. J. F. Eschscholtz, a surgeon and naturalist who came to the Pacific coast of North America with Russian expeditions in 1816 and 1824.

Annual
Slopes, plains, foothills
February to May
4500 to 6500 ft.

## BLUE GILIA
*Ipomopsis longiflora*
Phlox Family (Polemoniaceae)

Blue Gilia, with its very long, slender, pale blue floral tube, is one of the most beautiful species in this genus. The flowers look delicate, but grow in harsh environments with sandy or rocky soils. This is a great plant to add to your butterfly or hummingbird garden. *Ipomopsis* (you may know some of these species by the genus name, *Gilia*) is a Southwestern genus with over 25 species.

Annual or biennial
Dry plains, mesas, roadsides
Flowers May to October
3000 to 8000 ft.

### NUTTALL'S LINANTHUS
*Linanthus nuttallii*
Phlox Family (Polemoniaceae)

This prolific bloomer is common on sandy and gravelly soils of the grasslands and open ponderosa forests. The flowers are clustered at the tops of the stems. White petals surround a yellowish corolla tube, giving the appearance of an "eye." The leaves are opposite, but appear to be whorled around the stem. This plant species is named for Thomas Nuttall, an English botanist who collected in the Mississippi-Missouri River drainages. He described many new species, and several plants are named for him.

Perennial with woody base, almost shrubby
Open pine forests and dry stream beds
Flowers July to October
5500 to 10,000 ft.

### DESERT OR MOUNTAIN PHLOX
*Phlox austromontana*
Phlox Family (Polemoniaceae)

The Greek word phlox means "flame," and refers to the brilliantly colored flowers. A characteristic that helps in identifying the phlox family can be seen in the flower buds: the petals are folded so that the edge of one overlaps the edge of the next. The Desert or Mountain Phlox grows as a short, matted cluster, from a woody base, and is an attractive ground cover.

Perennial
Dry, often rocky, open areas of mountains
Flowers in June & July
6000 to 8000 ft.

### ORANGE MOSS ROSE
*Portulaca suffrutescens*
Purslane Family (Portulacaceae)

Orange Moss Rose looks like a flower of the tropics, not the xeric Southwest. The fleshy, succulent leaves are round in cross section. *Portulaca* means "carry milk," and refers to the milky juice in the stems. *Suffrutescens* means "woody," and refers to the slight woodiness at the base of the plant. Orange Moss Rose has beautiful coppery-orange petals surrounding yellow stamens. It makes a great ground cover, and is definitely the showiest of our native *Portulacas.* It prefers dry, sandy soil and full sun.

Perennial, slightly woody at base
Plains and mesas, dry rocky hills
Flowers July to September
3000 to 6000 ft.

## ABERT'S WILD BUCKWHEAT
*Eriogonum abertianum*
Buckwheat Family (Polygonaceae)

There are many species of wild buckwheats in the Southwest, and this is one of the most beautiful. The flowers are small, but occur in large clusters. The petal-like sepals are white or yellow, tinged with pink or red. Its flowers are followed by three-angled seeds (characteristic of the buckwheat family), which are eaten by rodents. Many species in the genus *Eriogonum* are woody, and when they are fruiting in the fall, may turn a beautiful red color.

Annual or biennial
March to September
Dry, sandy hills and mesas
3500 to 8000 ft.

## DESERT PAINTBRUSH
*Castilleja chromosa*
Snapdragon Family (Scrophulariaceae)

Paintbrushes are bright and easy to identify, even for beginners. But there is a lot of confusion about them. Paintbrushes have inconspicuous, almost hidden flowers. The color comes from their flower bracts and upper leaves, which are usually bright red to orange, but are pink or yellow in a few species. Many *Castillejas* are partially parasitic on the roots of other plants. *Castilleja chromosa* removes selenium from the soil, and so may be poisonous to livestock.

Perennial
Piñon-Juniper woodlands and sagebrush
Flowers April to June
3000 to 8000 ft.

## WHOLELEAF PAINTBRUSH
*Castilleja integra*
Snapdragon Family (Scrophulariaceae)

*Castilleja integra* is probably the Southwest's most common and widespread Paintbrush, growing over a wide range of elevations. Paintbrushes are named for the Spanish botanist, Castillejo. Scrophulariaceae is a big, beautiful family, and besides the paintbrushes, includes popular flowers such as figworts, snapdragons, monkeyflowers, penstemons, foxgloves, and more.

Perennial
Dry, rocky slopes
Flowers May to October
4500 to 10,500 ft.

## ROCKY MOUNTAIN COLUMBINE
### *Aquilegia coerulea*
Buttercup Family (Ranunculaceae)

Rocky Mountain Columbine, the state flower of Colorado, is a stunning beauty of high elevations. Like the mountains, its range extends into Arizona and New Mexico. Aven Nelson, a botanist in the Rockies, called this species the "queen of columbines." The large flowers have white petal blades with long blue or lavender spurs, and petal-like blue sepals. *Coerulea* means "blue." Long-tongued insects and humming-birds feed at nectaries in the spurs.

Perennial
Aspen forests, tundra
Blooms June to July
7000 to 12,000 ft.

## YELLOW COLUMBINE
### *Aquilegia chrysantha*
Buttercup Family (Ranunculaceae)

You're more likely to encounter the Yellow Columbine than the Rocky Mountain Columbine pictured above, and it's every bit as beautiful. *Aquilegia chrysantha* is the most abundant and widely distrib-uted of the Southwestern columbines, because it has such a wide altitudinal range. Every part of this flower is canary yellow: sepals, petals, and long, backward-pointing spurs.

Perennial
Moist slopes and canyons, shady forests
Flowers April to September
4000 to 11,000 ft.

## SCARLET PENSTEMON
### *Penstemon barbatus*
Snapdragon Family (Scrophulariaceae)

Scarlet Penstemon is a common flower with uncom-mon beauty. Its slender, bright scarlet flowers droop gracefully, and it grows up to three feet tall. Even during droughts, this penstemon can be seen flowering on the roadsides of the Southwest. It is pollinated by hummingbirds. The Navajo use *Penstemon barbatus* as medicine for humans and other animals. In the past, they boiled the flowers to make a sweet drink.

Perennial
Roadsides, Piñon-Juniper oak woods and
coniferous forests
Flowers June to October
4000 to 9,000 ft.

## NARROWLEAF PENSTEMON
*Penstemon linarioides*
Snapdragon Family (Scrophulariaceae)

There are dozens of species of penstemons in the Southwest, and all are beautiful. The genus name, *Penstemon*, means "five stamens." Penstemons have two pairs of fertile stamens. A fifth sterile stamen, called a staminode, is hairy, or "bearded," leading to the common name, "beardtongue." Narrowleaf Penstemon has lavender petals with purple veins, and a whitish flower throat with yellow hairs. Its leaves are grayish green and very narrow.

Perennial
Dry slopes and clearings in woodlands and pine forests
Flowers June to August
4500 to 9000 ft.

## ARIZONA PENSTEMON
*Penstemon pseudospectabilis*
Snapdragon Family (Scrophulariaceae)

Wooton and Standley, early New Mexico botanists, called Arizona Penstemon *Penstemon spectabilis*, meaning "spectacular penstemon." Since the name *P. spectabilis* had already been applied to a California Penstemon, the name of the Arizona penstemon was changed to *P. pseudospectabilis*, but it is no less beautiful. The flowers are large, funnel-shaped, and bright pinkish-red. The upper pairs of leaves are united around the stem, so that it appears the stem is growing right up through the leaves. Arizona Penstemon grows to three feet tall.

Perennial
Dry, rocky slopes and canyons
Flowers April to June
4000 to 7000 ft.

## SACRED DATURA
*Datura wrightii*
Nightshade Family (Solanaceae)

Sacred Datura is a fabulous plant for a night garden! The huge, trumpet-shaped flowers open at night, releasing their intoxicating perfume. Because they are white (tinged with purple), pollinating sphinx moths can spot the flowers even on a moonless night. The flowers close during the hot part of the day. The fruits are large, round, prickly seed capsules, hence the common name, Thorn Apple. In Spanish, Datura is called *Toloache* (toe low AH chay). All parts of the plant are very poisonous if ingested.

Perennial
Sandy soils, roadsides, deserts, woodlands
Flowers June to October
3000 to 6500 ft.

### ROCKY MOUNTAIN IRIS
*Iris missouriensis*
Iris Family (Iridaceae)

The word *Iris* comes from the Greek *iridos*, meaning "rainbow," and is given to this flower for its many colors. In the Southwest, *Iris missouriensis* is our only native Iris. Though smaller, it looks quite similar to the cultivated species. Its flower structure and color is unusual: three white and purple petals stand up, and three petal-like sepals, blue, yellow and white, curve downward. Rocky Mountain Iris attracts butterflies. The Navajo used it in ceremonies and as a green dye.

Perennial
Wet meadows and damp forest clearings
Flowers May to September
6000 to 10,500 feet

### NODDING ONION
*Allium cernuum*
Lily Family (Liliaceae)

There are many wild onions in the Southwest, and Nodding Onion is probably the most common and widespread. Its pale pink flowers are arranged in umbels, as are the flowers of the other onions. *Cernuum* means "nodding," and this feature of the flowers distinguishes this species from the others. Onion, garlic, chive, leeks and shallots all belong to the genus *Allium*. Many animals, including Montezuma Quails, eat the bulbs, which can also be used in cooking.

Perennial
Open slopes and meadows
Flowers July to October
6500 to 9000 feet

### MARIPOSA LILY
*Calochortus ambiguus*
Lily Family (Liliaceae)

Mariposa Lily is a beautiful wildflower, tulip-like in appearance. It has white petals, with a distinctive gland toward the bottom of the petals. *Calochortus* means "beautiful grass." Of course, this species is not a grass, but like the grasses, it IS a monocot. All of the plants on this page are monocots, with parallel-veined leaves, and flower parts in threes or multiples of three. (See page 185 for more about monocots.) *Calochortus ambiguus* is the most widely distributed of all the Arizona mariposas. In Spanish, these flowers are called *mariposa*, which means butterfly.

Perennial
Dry slopes
Flowers May to August
5000 to 8000 feet

# GYMNOSPERMS

If one could time travel back 290 million years, gymnosperms would be one of the few familiar sights. These plants have been on Earth for a long time, and were the first to produce seeds. The fossil record indicates that the abundance and diversity of the gymnosperms is much less now than in the past. The word "gymnosperm" comes from two Greek words meaning "naked seed." The seeds of gymnosperms are exposed, unlike those of the more recently evolved angiosperms or flowering plants, which are enclosed in fruits.

The conifers, or cone-producing plants, comprise the largest division of gymnosperms. Most conifers are commonly known as evergreens, because they retain their leaves all winter. In the southwestern United States, familiar conifers include the pines, junipers, firs and spruces. These trees have benefitted humans in numerous way, providing food, medicine, timber, fuel, jewelry (amber), dyes and of course, beauty.

In the arid Southwest, another common gymnosperm is the Joint Fir or Mormon Tea (genus *Ephedra*). Although the Joint Fir looks nothing like a conifer, it shares some of its characteristics. Most botanists consider *Ephedra* to be an evolutionary intermediary between the conifers and the flowering plants. Research has demonstrated a quite distinctive evolution of the Joint Firs from true conifers. All the *Ephedras* in New Mexico are shrubs, thought to have evolved much more recently than the true conifers, and the leaves are scale-like and opposite (two at each node) or whorled (three at each node.) When you have an opportunity, stop and take a good look at this unique and somewhat rare example of evolutionary history.

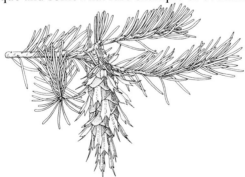

"If you are thriftily inclined, you will find pines congenial company, for, unlike the hand-to-mouth hardwoods, they never pay current bills out of current earnings; they live solely on their savings of the year before. In fact every pine carries an open bankbook, in which his cash balance is eroded by 30 June of each year."

Aldo Leopold, *Sand County Almanac*

76

## ARIZONA CYPRESS, CEDRO
*Cupressus arizonica*
Cypress Family (Cupressaceae)

An attractive evergreen tree with its round, woody cones, Arizona Cypress is planted for ornament, windbreaks, and erosion control. The wood is lightweight, straw-colored and has a pleasant odor; its durability makes it useful for fenceposts. According to Donald Culross Peattie, Arizona Cypress was favored as a Christmas tree in the 1950s, because its needles didn't shed as easily as firs and the cones could be gilded for use as ornaments. Seeds may be planted in the spring, and will germinate more successfully in deep sandy loam. Arizona Cypress may also be propagated by cuttings. It grows quickly in good soil and may live to 700 years old. A tincture of fresh twigs was used by Native Americans to treat all skin fungus infections including ringworm and athlete's foot. A vapor of burning leaves was once used to aid in childbirth and to help remove the afterbirth. Baked stems were applied to burns and other damaged skin areas. Pounded leaves can be chewed to relieve toothaches.

**DESCRIPTION: Height** of this evergreen tree to 24 m (80 ft.), with a diameter of up to 1.5 m (5 ft.); **bark** of smaller limbs smooth but shredding with age to expose a dark red inner bark, older trunks dark brown and broken into irregular squarish plates; **leaves** small, awl-like or scale-like, blue-green; **seed cones** at maturity dry and woody, orbicular, commonly more than 1.5 cm (0.5 in.) in diameter, composed of 6 to 8 distinct warty–surfaced scales, opening by several sutures at maturity, or after a fire, persistent on the branches several years, long after seeds have fallen.

**DISTRIBUTION:** The range of Arizona Cypress barely touches southwest New Mexico, but is abundant in southeastern Arizona. It occurs in California, western Texas and northern Mexico.

**HABITAT:** Dry, well-drained sunny slopes at 5,000 to 7,000 ft. (1,520 to 2,230 m) in elevation.

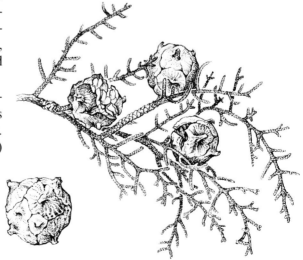

## COMMON JUNIPER, DWARF JUNIPER
*Juniperus communis*
Cypress Family (Cupressaceae)

Common Juniper deserves its name, since it is the most widespread of all the junipers. Because of its shrubby habit, Common Juniper works well in a rock garden, along walls, or where a low evergreen is desired. It thrives in moist, cool, shady environments and is hardy once fully established. Over thirty species of birds and many small mammals eat the berries, and deer browse the foliage. The berries of this juniper are the principal flavoring agents in gin and alcoholic bitters. They can also be roasted and used as a coffee substitute, albeit a poor one. The juniper berry oil is used as a diuretic for mild urinary tract infections, to induce menstruation, and to treat kidney complaints, snakebite and intestinal worms. A poultice of needles and twigs can be used to treat wounds. To stimulate digestion, and for recovering alcoholics whose digestive systems are impaired, several berries are chewed before eating. The wood is burned for incense in India, and can also be used as a fumigant.

**DESCRIPTION: Height** of this evergreen shrub to 1 m (3 ft.); branches appearing flattened from above, often forming circular patches; **leaves** awl-shaped and sharp-pointed needles, occurring in whorls of three at right angles to the branches; **seed cones** are dark blue and berry-like, covered with a waxy bloom, bearing 1 to 3 seeds.

**DISTRIBUTION:** Northern mountains of New Mexico, north to Colorado and Canada, west to Arizona, Oregon, Washington and California.

**HABITAT:** Well-drained soil on sunny sites, at high altitudes of 8,000 to 11,500 ft.(2,440 to 3,510 m).

## ALLIGATOR JUNIPER
*Juniperus deppeana*
Cypress Family (Cupressaceae)
**Related Species: One-Seeded Juniper,** *Juniperus monosperma*

Don't let the familiar nature of Alligator Juniper discourage you from using it as an ornamental. It is attractive at all stages of growth: bluish-green as a young tree, becoming dark green and quite tall, an excellent provider of shade. Even half-dead, Alligator Junipers are picturesque: dead limbs often remain on the trees, giving them a grotesque yet beautiful appearance. *Juniperus deppeana* is the largest of all the southwestern junipers, and one of the largest of them all grows in Fort Bayard, New Mexico. Alligator Juniper is slow-growing, long-lived, and can sprout from stumps. Its leaves are browsed by livestock and deer, and the fruit is eaten by gray fox, black bear, coyote, rock squirrel and wild turkey. If you are one of the many people in the Southwest who suffer allergic reactions to the juniper's pollen, make sure you don't plant a male tree. In Chihuahua, Mexico, Alligator Juniper's leaves are used as a remedy for rheumatism. Other cultures have also traditionally used juniper for medicinal purposes, but it wasn't until the 20th century that antibiotics were isolated from the leaves. The bark of *Juniperus deppeana*, with its squarish plates, is said to resemble the back of an alligator, hence its common name. This feature distinguishes it easily from One-Seeded Juniper, *Juniperus monosperma*, which has shreddy bark.

**DESCRIPTION: Height** of this large evergreen tree to 12 m (40 ft.) or more; **bark** of older branches and trunk divided into squarish plates; **leaves** bluish-green and scale-like; **pollen and seed cones** borne on separate trees; pollen cones inconspicuous, seed cones berry-like, bluish-green, maturing in the second year and turning brown and leathery.

**DISTRIBUTION:** Most common in the central and southern portions of New Mexico, Alligator Juniper occurs throughout the state. It is also found in the high mountains of western Texas, south to Chihuahua and Sonora, and west to Arizona.

**HABITAT:** Dry sites at elevations from 6,000 to 8,000 ft. (1,830 to 2,440 m), often found growing with piñons, oaks, other junipers, and Ponderosa Pine.

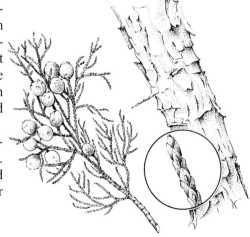

# ONE-SEEDED JUNIPER
*Juniperus monosperma*
Cypress Family (Cupressaceae)
**Related Species: Alligator Juniper,** *Juniperus deppeana*

One-seeded Juniper has attractive shredding bark, distinguishing it from Alligator Juniper's checkered bark. This plant generally grows as a many-stemmed shrub, but can be pruned into a small tree. It is well suited to dry, alkaline soils. Much of *Juniperus monosperma* was used by Native Americans: bark was woven into mats and saddles, fruits were ground into flour, bark and berries were used for dyes, the wood was used for fence posts, firewood and building hogans. In times of food shortage, the Navajo ate the inner bark, and also cut off branches for their sheep to eat when snow was deep. The shredding bark makes good kindling for campfires, and the wood burns well and has a pleasant odor. The fruits are eaten by many birds and mammals. A tea of dried leaves and berries is used to treat bladder infections. A couple of berries can be chewed to help in digestion for older people and for those whose digestion is impaired due to alcohol abuse.

**DESCRIPTION: Height** of evergreen, many-stemmed shrub, (sometimes a small tree) to 8 m (25 ft.); **twigs** reddish brown, becoming gray and stringy with age; **bark** shredding; **leaves** scale-like, gray-green; **pollen and seed cones** borne on separate trees, pollen cones inconspicuous, seed cones on female trees are berry-like, copper-colored to blue-black and contain one seed.

**DISTRIBUTION:** Widespread in New Mexico, occurring east to western Texas and Oklahoma, north to Colorado, Utah, Wyoming and Nevada, west to Arizona and south to Mexico.

**HABITAT:** Dry hills and mesas 5,000 to 8,000 ft. (1,520 to 2,440 m) in elevation, often found growing with Piñon Pine.

**CONSERVATION CONSIDERATIONS:** One-seeded Juniper increases with overgrazing, and is sometimes cleared, along with Piñon Pine, to create better grazing lands.

## ROCKY MOUNTAIN JUNIPER
*Juniperus scopulorum*
Cypress Family (Cupressaceae)
**Related Species: One-seeded Juniper,** *Juniperus monosperma*

Because of its drooping or "weeping" form, this graceful juniper makes a good ornamental. Rocky Mountain Juniper is slow-growing, long-lived, and has slightly higher water requirements than the other junipers. Plants can be started from seed or from cuttings. Along with the other junipers, this species is used for food and cover for many mammals and birds. The durable wood is used for fuel and fence posts, and because it has the characteristic "cedar" odor, it is also made into cedar chests and other specialty products. Native Americans used the shredding bark for bedding. Juniper leaves have been used in the treatment of rheumatism.

**DESCRIPTION: Height** of this small tree may reach 8 m (25 ft.); **bark** reddish to gray-brown and shredding; younger branches drooping at the ends; **leaves** dark or gray-green, scale-like; **pollen and seed cones** growing on separate trees, pollen cones inconspicuous, seed cones on female trees are pea-sized, blue and berry-like, maturing in the second year, generally containing two seeds.

**DISTRIBUTION:** Common over the northern two-thirds of New Mexico, west to Arizona, Utah and Nevada, east to the Dakotas, Oklahoma and western Texas, north to Colorado, Oregon,Washington and Canada.

**HABITAT:** Mountain slopes, canyon bottoms in sandy or gravelly soil, dry exposed mesas, cliff faces at elevations of 6,500 to 9,000 ft. (1,980 to 2,740 m).

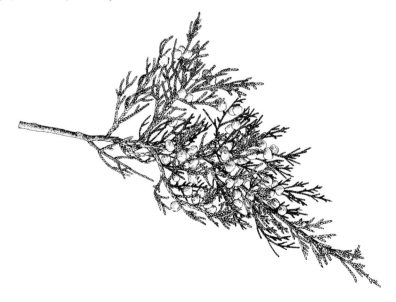

# WHITE FIR, BALSAM FIR
*Abies concolor*
Pine Family (Pinaceae)
**Related Species: Subalpine Fir,** *Abies lasiocarpa*

*Abies concolor* grows in the warmest and driest climate of all the native firs. Growing rapidly when young and later slowing, it may attain an age of 350 years. It is resistant to fire, heat and drought. White firs are often planted as ornamentals and for use as Christmas trees. Because of their pleasant aroma, firs have sometimes been used as a stuffing material for pillows, and for scenting soaps, oils and shampoos. Native Americans used White Fir twigs to make pipe stems, and treated cuts with the resinous pitch. White Fir cones disintegrate, often with the help of squirrels, while still attached to the tree, so whole cones are not usually seen on the ground. The seeds are readily eaten by squirrels, grouse and other birds, and the young growth is browsed by deer and mountain sheep. Wildlife also utilize White Fir for cover.

**DESCRIPTION: Height** of this evergreen tree to 30 m (100 ft.) or more with a trunk diameter up to 1 m (3 ft.); young trees generally symmetrical and conical, older trees becoming irregular or rounded; twigs exhibit smooth round scars after needles fall off; **bark** of young firs smooth and gray to white, becoming gray, thick and furrowed with age; **leaves** needle-like, averaging 6 cm (1.25 in.) in length, crowded on the branches, pale bluish green or silvery blue, sharp at the tips, and flat; **seed cones** grayish-green, 7 to 12 cm (3 to 5 in.) long, perched upright on the higher limbs.

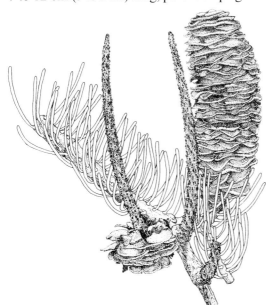

**DISTRIBUTION:** Western two-thirds of New Mexico, west to Arizona, Utah, California, and Oregon, north to Colorado and Wyoming, south to Sonora and Chihuahua.

**HABITAT:** Coniferous forests of the low mountains, usually on north-facing slopes at elevations of 7,000 to 9,000 ft. (2,130 to 2,770 m).

## COLORADO BLUE SPRUCE, SILVER SPRUCE
*Picea pungens*
Pine Family (Pinaceae)
**Related Species: Engelmann Spruce,** *Picea engelmannii*

Blue Spruce is the State tree of both Colorado and Utah, and is much sought after as a Christmas tree. Fortune seekers during the gold rush often returned with a "silver" spruce instead of gold, and planted it in the Midwest, where it is still seen today. The specific name, *pungens*, means "sharp-pointed" and refers to the leaves. If you grab a branch of Colorado Blue Spruce, you'll feel the stiff and prickly needles. Spruces are long-lived, slow-growing and wind-resistant. Their seeds are eaten by many species of birds and the foliage is browsed by deer.

**DESCRIPTION: Height** of evergreen tree may reach 30 m (100 ft.) with a trunk diameter of up to 1 m (3 ft.); young trees symmetrical, older trees losing their lower boughs and becoming pole-like; **bark** of young trees pale gray and smooth, older bark gray to reddish brown and deeply divided into broad ridges; twigs rough after needles fall off (a short needle stalk remains on the twig after the needles have fallen); **leaves** are needles, mostly 4-sided, arranged in a spiral around the twig, silvery white to light or dark bluish-green, sharp to the touch, almost spine-tipped; **seed cones** to 10 cm (4 in.) long, chestnut-brown, hanging down from (usually) upper branches.

Engelmann Spruce grows taller (to 40 m) than Colorado Blue Spruce, and at higher elevations. Also, its needles are not sharp and prickly like the needles of Colorado Blue Spruce, and its seed cones are smaller (to 7 cm).

**DISTRIBUTION:** Colorado Blue Spruce grows in mountainous portions of New Mexico, Colorado, Idaho, Montana, Arizona and Utah. Engelmann Spruce occurs in higher elevations scattered throughout New Mexico, in the western states, and into Canada and Mexico.

**HABITAT:** Colorado Blue Spruce grows in mixed conifer and ponderosa pine forests, in moist valley bottoms and along stream banks at elevations from 7,200 to 10,500 ft. (2,200 to 3,200 m). Engelmann Spruce occurs in montane and subalpine forests over 8,000 ft. (2,400 m).

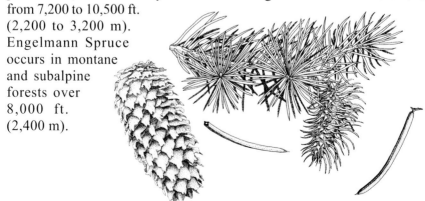

## COLORADO BRISTLECONE or FOXTAIL PINE
*Pinus aristata*
Pine Family (Pineaceae)
**Related Species: Intermountain Bristlecone Pine**, *Pinus longaeva*

At timberline, trees are often weighed down by snow and ice, and whipped by the wind. The stunted, gnarled growth that results is called *krummholz*, or "crooked wood." Bristlecone Pine, at timberline, exhibits this form, but at lower elevations, it is a symmetrical, more conventional tree. It is very cold- and drought-tolerant, and often retains its leaves for fifteen to thirty years. These needles grow very densely on the tips of the twigs, earning this tree one of its common names, Foxtail Pine. *Pinus aristata* grows very slowly, taking up to ten years to add one mm to its trunk diameter. Rodents, including porcupines, find the seeds to be a tasty treat.

**DESCRIPTION: Height** of evergreen tree to 15 m (50 ft.), growing as a shrub at timberline; **bark** thin and grayish-white when tree is young, becoming red-brown and shallowly ridged with age; **leaves** are needles in clusters or fascicles of 5, curved, with gray-green resin spots, sticky to the touch, up to 4 cm (1.5 in.) long, densely crowded at the tips of the twigs; **seed cones** are purplish-brown, cone scales with prickles, up to 9 cm (3.5 in.) long.

**DISTRIBUTION:** Northern New Mexico, north to Colorado, west to Arizona.

**HABITAT:** Exposed areas on dry, rocky soils in upper montane to subalpine zones to timberline at elevations of 9,500 to 12,500 ft. (2,900 to 3,810 m).

## PINYON PINE
*Pinus edulis*
Pine Family (Pinaceae)
**Related Species: Mexican Piñon,** *Pinus cembroides*

Piñon Pine, New Mexico's state tree, is very slow-growing and long lived (up to 250 years). *Edulis* means edible, a very appropriate name for this tree. Its cones produce the tasty and popular Piñon or pine nuts, which are eagerly collected by humans, smaller mammals, and birds. Piñon ranks first in desirability among nut trees not under cultivation. The Piñon is a very resinous tree, and Native Americans have used the resin for caulk, to make woven baskets watertight, and as a dye. Traditionally, the wood of Piñon Pine has been used as a structural timber in southwestern pit houses. Today, small piñons are often cut for Christmas trees, although this is surely not their best use. The needles of *Pinus edulis* are longer than those of *Pinus cembroides*, and usually occur in clusters of two instead of three.

**DESCRIPTION: Height** of evergreen tree or shrub to 11 m (37 ft.); **leaves** needle-like, usually 2 to the cluster or fascicle, blue-green to yellowish-green, stiff, sharp-pointed, up to 5 cm (2 in.) in length; **pollen cones** dark red, covering the tree, **seed cones** on the ends of the twigs becoming yellowish-brown, up to 5 cm (2 in.) long, maturing in the second year.

**DISTRIBUTION:** Widespread in New Mexico, north to southern Colorado and Wyoming, west to Arizona, Utah and Nevada, east to western Texas, south to Mexico.

**HABITAT:** Dry, rocky places, often associated with junipers, oaks or Ponderosa Pine, at elevations of 4,500 to 8,000 ft. (1,370 to 2,440 m).

# LIMBER PINE
*Pinus flexilis*
Pine Family (Pinaceae)
**Related Species: Southwestern White Pine,** *Pinus strobiformis*
**Ponderosa Pine,** *Pinus ponderosa*

If you need a tree for a dry, windy site, consider planting a Limber Pine. They are rather slow-growing and long-lived, and because of their tolerance to dry and windy sites, can survive where other pines cannot. Limber Pine's branches can often be bent double without breaking, allowing them to withstand severe winds and snow loads. The young twigs are so supple they can sometimes be tied into knots without breaking! Squirrels, chipmunks, piñon jays and magpies eat the seeds, and the foliage is browsed by mule deer and elk. Freshly cut wood smells like turpentine.

**DESCRIPTION: Height** of evergreen tree to 26 m (80 ft.); crown conic, becoming rounded with age; **bark** smooth and gray on young trees, becoming ridged with age; **leaves** needle-like, 3 to 7 cm (1 to 3 in.) long, dark green, pliant, five to a fascicle, bunched at the ends of the twigs; **pollen and seed cones** borne on the same tree, pollen cones yellowish or reddish, borne on spikes throughout the crown of the tree, seed cones tan, maturing in two years, up to 15 cm (6 in.) in length, borne in clusters at the ends of the upper branches.

**DISTRIBUTION:** Northern mountainous portion of New Mexico, in Arizona, Utah, Idaho, Oregon, Montana, Nevada, California, Colorado, Wyoming, North and South Dakota, Nebraska and Canada.

**HABITAT:** Dry, rocky, windswept slopes in the high mountains near treeline, in Douglas Fir and Spruce-Fir forests, at 7,500 to 12,000 ft. (2,290 to 3,660 m) in elevation.

### Limber Pine versus Southwestern White Pine

Where their ranges overlap, Limber and Southwestern White Pines reportedly hybridize, making them difficult to distinguish. The following two characteristics can help to differentiate the two species: Limber Pine's needles are slightly shorter than those of Southwestern White Pine (3-7 cm vs. 4-9 cm). Southwestern White Pine's cones have scales that are strongly reflexed toward the base, and the cones of Limber Pine lack this feature.

## SOUTHWESTERN WHITE PINE
*Pinus strobiformis*
Pine Family (Pinaceae)
**Related Species: Limber Pine,** *Pinus flexilis*
                        **Ponderosa Pine,** *Pinus ponderosa*

     Southwestern White Pine is one of our least known white pines. Though it is fairly common in southern New Mexico, it grows in relatively inaccessible places. If you don't look carefully, you can mistake it for Ponderosa Pine, which it resembles in bark and growth habit. *Pinus strobiformis* has shorter, thinner needles than *Pinus ponderosa*, and its cones are much longer, with scales that are turned back. Southwestern White Pine is a high elevation tree, and its branches are able to withstand high winds and heavy snow loads without breaking. Squirrels, chipmunks, and birds eat the seeds, and the foliage is browsed by mule deer and elk. The seed cones mature in two years, shed their seeds, and then fall from the tree.

**DESCRIPTION: Height** of evergreen tree to about 30 m (100 ft.), trunk to almost 1 m (3 ft.) in diameter; tree slender and straight in profile, crown conic, becoming rounded in maturity; **bark** gray on young trees, becoming red brown and furrowed with age; **leaves** are needles 4-9 cm (1.5 to 3.5 in.) long, bluish green, pliant, five to a fascicle; **pollen and seed cones** borne on the same tree, pollen cones pale yellow-brown, seed cones yellow to light brown, 5 to 25 cm ( 2 to 10 in.) long, with scales strongly reflexed toward the base, maturing in two years.

**DISTRIBUTION:** Common in the southern, especially the southwestern, counties of New Mexico, and in Arizona, west Texas, and Mexico.

**HABITAT:** Arid to moist high mountains and montane forests, from 6,500 to 9,500 ft. (1,980 to 2,900 m).

LIMBER PINE
*Pinus flexilis*
(left)

SOUTHWESTERN
WHITE PINE
*Pinus strobiformis*
(right)

# PONDEROSA PINE, WESTERN YELLOW PINE
*Pinus ponderosa* var. *scopulorum*
Pine Family (Pinaceae)
**Related Species: Arizona Yellow Pine,** *Pinus ponderosa* var. *arizonica*

Ponderosa, the most widely distributed pine in North America, provides cover for wildlife. Elk and other wild game of the higher mountains winter in the Ponderosas. Young trees are browsed by deer, elk and Barbary sheep; bears enjoy the immature trees' inner bark. Squirrels eat the shoots of older trees and the seeds. Wild turkey use Ponderosas for food and shelter. Donald Peattie, in his book, *A Natural History of Western Trees*, states that Ponderosas "cover an area of 1,000,000 square miles on this planet's surface!" Ponderosa Pines may live for up to 500 years if they are growing in an area too steep or remote to log easily, as this species is used extensively for lumber. Because of vigorous root growth, Ponderosas can tolerate drier sites than many other conifers. The two varieties of Ponderosa are distinguished by the number of needles per fascicle: variety *scopulorum* has two-three needles, and variety *arizonica* has three-five needles.

**DESCRIPTION: Height** of this evergreen tree to 20 m (67 ft.) or more, with a trunk diameter to 1 m (3 ft.), trunks straight with a high open crown; **bark** on young trees very dark brown, becoming thick, lighter in color, separating into cinnamon-brown scales or flat plates; **leaves** needle-like, 11 to 22 cm (4.25 to 8.5 in.) in length, usually three in a fascicle (rarely two or five), dark green, thick and flexible; **pollen and seed cones** occurring on the same tree, pollen cones red to yellow, seed cones dark red, in pairs or clustered, becoming light reddish brown, 6 to 9 cm (2.5 to 3.5 in.) in length, scales with short recurved prickles.

**DISTRIBUTION:** Widespread in New Mexico, north to Colorado and Canada, west to Arizona, California and the mountainous regions of the western states, east to west Texas, south to Mexico's mountains. Arizona Yellow Pine is confined to the southwest corner of New Mexico, southeast Arizona and adjacent Mexico.

**HABITAT:** Montane to subalpine ecosystems at 6,500 to 9,500 ft. (1,980 to 2,900 m) in elevation. Ponderosa Pine can be found with junipers, Piñon Pine, and Gambel Oak in lower elevations, and with mixed conifers at higher elevations.

**CONSERVATION CONSIDERATIONS:** Fire suppression enables thickets of "dog hair" - young, spindly pines - to become dense stands of small trees that burn hot and fast, and spread wildfire to larger, older trees that might otherwise have withstood fires. Old, thick-barked Ponderosas may survive twenty to thirty fires in their lifetimes.

## DOUGLAS FIR
*Pseudotsuga menziesii* var. *glauca*
Pine Family (Pinaceae)
**Synonym**: *Pseudotsuga taxifolia*

Douglas Fir is not a true fir, despite the common name. True firs have erect cones, while those of Douglas Fir hang down from the branches. Its seeds are eaten by squirrels, chipmunks and grouse, and the foliage is browsed by deer. Douglas Fir's principal value to wildlife is as cover. Second in height only to redwoods, Douglas Fir is an important timber tree, providing more lumber than any other American tree. And like redwoods, *Pseudotsuga menziesii* is long-lived, surviving 500 to 1,000 years. Douglas Fir can be most easily distinguished from other conifers by its cones, which have three pointed bracts. This species does well in sun or shade, and can withstand high winds. The needles of Douglas Fir can be steeped in hot water to make a tea high in vitamin C, and the bud tips are chewed for mouth sores.

**DESCRIPTION:** **Height** of evergreen tree may reach 40 m (133 ft.) or more, trunk diameter 1 m (3 ft.) or more, with a pyramidal crown and drooping lower branches; **bark** of young trees whitish gray and smooth, becoming furrowed with age, cinnamon-brown and very thick; **leaves** are needles flattened and blunt at the ends, dark green, 2 to 3 cm (0.75 to 1 in.) long, with a groove on the upper side and a slight stalk (petiole); **seed and pollen cones** occurring on the same tree, pollen cones orange-red, seed cones green or reddish-purple, becoming brown with age, hanging down from the branches, to 10 cm (4 in.) long, cone scales have three points (middle one is longer) or each bract.

**DISTRIBUTION:** Relatively abundant in the foothills and mountains of New Mexico, west to Arizona, north to Canada, south to Mexico, east to west Texas.

**HABITAT:** Mixed coniferous forests, above Ponderosa Pines and below spruces, often found on north-facing slopes from 6,500 ft. (1,980 m) to almost treeline.

# MORMON TEA, TORREY JOINT-FIR and BIG JOINT-FIR
*Ephedra torreyana* and *Ephedra trifurca*
Joint-Fir Family (Ephedraceae)

*Ephedras* can be identified by their skeleton-like appearance and spine-tipped yellow branches. The stems are photosynthetic, and this plant is wind-pollinated. Although *Ephedras* are gymnosperms ("naked seeds") by definition, most authorities place their evolution between the true conifers and the angiosperms, or flowering plants. The drug *ephedrine* comes from the roots and stems of an *Ephedra* from China. The species of *Ephedra* that grow in North America contain little or no *ephedrine*, but can still be used medicinally. They are used to stimulate respiration and prevent asthma and hay fever. Native Americans and early settlers brewed a very strong *Ephedra* tea for treatment of syphilis and other diseases and as a stomach tonic. It is used as a diuretic and for mild kidney inflammations. Some medical practitioners now question the safety of *Ephedra*. The branches yield dyes of tan, peach and gray. Mountain sheep, bighorns, and jackrabbits browse this plant, and the seeds are eaten by scaled quail. In emergencies, cattle will also graze *Ephedras*.

**DESCRIPTION: Height** of erect shrub to 1 m (3 ft.); [*E. trifurca* to 4 m (13 ft.)]; branches rigid, solitary or whorled at the nodes; young stems pale blue-green, almost smooth, becoming gray and irregularly fissured; **leaves** scale-like, 3 to 6 mm (less than 0.25 in.) in length, in threes, whorled around the stem; **pollen-bearing and seed-bearing strobili** (primitive cone-like structures) borne in spikes, bracts in many cycles of three, seed-bearing strobili are in tiny cones, solitary or in twos or threes, beaked, tan colored. Torrey Joint-fir is very similar in appearance to Big Joint-Fir. They can be distinguished by leaf length: averaging less than 5 mm and 9 mm (0.25 to 0.5 in.) or more, respectively. The terminal buds of *Ephedra torreyana* disintegrate early and are not spiny, while those of *Ephedra trifurca* are persistent and spiny. Big Joint-fir can reach a height of 4 m (13 ft.).

**DISTRIBUTION:** Torrey Joint-fir is common throughout central portion of New Mexico, but to be expected statewide, west to Arizona and Nevada, east to Texas, south to Chihuahua. Big Joint-fir grows in the southern third of New Mexico, in Arizona and California, west Texas, and Mexico.

**HABITAT:** Dry, rocky or sandy slopes, frequently growing in gypsum, at elevations from 3,300 to 6,000 ft. (1,010 to 1,830 m).

# ANGIOSPERMS

All plants with seeds are either gymnosperms or angiosperms. The previous section, the conifers and joint-firs, introduced the gymnosperms. All other plants in this book belong to the largest division of the Plant Kingdom: the angiosperms, or flowering plants. The fossil record suggests that flowering plants appeared on Earth about 135 million years ago, long after gymnosperms were well established.

## Diversity

Worldwide, there are an estimated 250,000 species of flowering plants, and this large number reflects their great diversity. If asked to picture a "typical" plant, most of us think of flowering plants, our familiar neighbors. Angiosperms live in almost every habitat on the planet, and range in size from tiny annuals to huge, long-lived trees.

## Dicots and Monocots

To break the large diversity of angiosperms into manageable groups, botanists commonly divide them into two major classes: Dicotyledoneae and Monocotyledoneae, or dicots and monocots. About 80 per cent of angiosperms are dicots. With the exception of the agaves and their allies, all the plants in the following sections are dicots.

While there are several differences between dicots and monocots, the following characteristics are easily observable. The leaves of dicots have netted venation, and monocots' leaves have parallel veins. (See page 200, Illustrated Glossary) Dicots have flower parts (petals, sepals, stamens) in 4s or 5s, while monocots' flower parts are in 3s or multiples of 3. Dicots have two embryonic leaves in their seeds (remember seeing two big leaves when a bean plant first emerges from the ground?); monocots have just one seed leaf.

## Flowers

All flowers share one function: producing a new generation. The diversity in floral sizes, shapes and structures is huge, making it difficult to describe a "typical" flower. Botanists use this variation, among other characters, for classification. Some flowers, like those of the grasses, are inconspicuous and wind-pollinated. Others are fragrant, showy and colorful, and attract insect, bird and mammal pollinators.

# Fruit

For botanists, the word "fruit" has a different meaning than it does in general usage. In the marketplace, fruits are sweet edibles; in botany, fruits are often inedible or even poisonous. Fruits develop from flowers, and contain the seeds that perpetuate the plants' existence. Unlike the gymnosperms with exposed seeds, the seeds of angiosperms are enclosed in fruits. In fact, the word angiosperm means "seeds in vessels." As with flowers, there is much variation in fruit types. Seeds and fruits have many methods of dispersal: some are moved by wind or water, others cling to animals or are eaten by them.

# Deciduous Plants

Deciduous plants are those that lose their leaves in the fall, and produce new leaves in the spring. Planting deciduous trees near your home works to your advantage, blocking the sun in the hot summer months, and allowing sunlight to warm your home in the winter. In the Southwest, most of our oaks employ a different strategy: they keep their leaves in the winter, and drop them in the spring. When there is sufficient moisture, they grow new leaves.

With the exception of some evergreen shrubs, the plants in the trees, shrubs and vines sections are all deciduous.

# TREES

Trees, more than any other plants (with the exception of food plants!), seem to become a part of our lives. Many of us have childhood memories that feature a particular tree or grove of trees. It's more unusual to become emotionally attached to grass or annual wildflowers, while we may appreciate their fleeting beauty.

Perhaps for this reason, trees are often the first plants that people learn to identify. Or maybe the stature of trees makes them difficult to ignore. In either case, beginning with trees is a good idea, since there are far fewer trees than shrubs or herbaceous wildflowers.

Trees are often used to define ecosystems: ecologists speak of piñon-juniper woodlands, and ponderosa pine or spruce-fir forests. Knowing the dominant tree species, we can make inferences about the other plant species we're likely to encounter and what animals inhabit the area. We can also make assumptions about elevational ranges and annual precipitation.

The tree species included in this section are native to riparian areas of the Southwest. They will do well in an arroyo, or where they receive roof runoff or other diverted water.

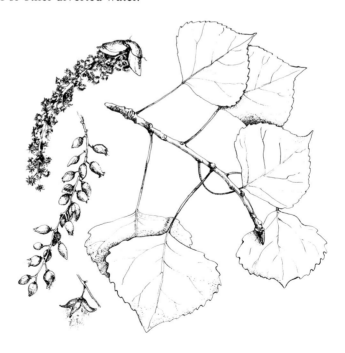

"... grasses murmur but a cottonwood seems to be the articulating of the tongueless wind: to take comfort in this garrulity is to use the sound and not let it go wasted."

William Least Heat-Moon, *Prairie Erth*, 1991

# BOX ELDER, FRESNO DE GUAJUCO
*Acer negundo*
Maple Family  (Aceraceae)
**Similar Species: Poison Ivy,** *Toxicodendron rydbergii*

An attractive riparian species, *Acer negundo* grows rapidly and makes a good ornamental and shade tree. Like other members of the Maple family, Box Elder can be tapped for sugar. In the fall, the leaves of Box Elder turn red and yellow, reminding us of its eastern relatives. *Acer negundo* is the only maple that has compound leaves; while it usually has only three leaflets, it sometimes has up to seven. When young, Box Elder's trifoliate leaf arrangement is easily confused with Poison Ivy's infamous three leaflets. Poison Ivy has white berries, and Box Elder has the samaras (or "keys") that are characteristic of the maple family. If the plant in question has leaves only, and no fruits, it's best to remember the old adage, "Leaves of three, leave it be." Box Elder seeds readily and also grows by suckers, so it can be difficult to control.

**DESCRIPTION: Height** of this deciduous shrub or tree to 20 m (67 ft.), with a broad rounded crown; **leaves** opposite, trifoliate or pinnately compound with 3 to 7 leaflets, averaging more than 12 cm (5 in.) in length, the lower surface hairy along the veins, leaflets coarsely serrate above the

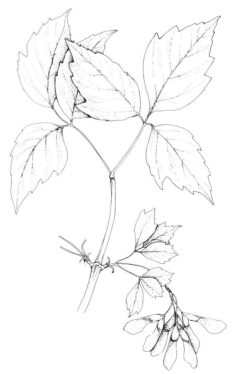

middle; new stems green to blue or gray in color, with age the trunk becoming rough and knobby; inflorescence a drooping raceme, male and female **flowers** occur on separate trees, appearing before or with the leaves; **fruit** a paired samara, 2 to 5 cm (0.75 to 2 in.) long.

**DISTRIBUTION:** Common throughout New Mexico, east to Texas, Oklahoma, Arkansas, Louisiana and Florida, north to Canada, west to Arizona, Nevada, California and Washington, south to Mexico.

**HABITAT:** Stream banks, floodplains and other moist areas from 5,200 to 7,500 ft. (1,600 to 2,300 m) in elevation.

## ARIZONA WALNUT, NOGAL SILVESTRE
*Juglans major*
Walnut Family (Juglandaceae)
**Related Species: Little Walnut,** *Juglans microcarpa*

The nuts of this species are enjoyed by squirrels and rodents, and can be eaten by people as well. In addition to providing food, Arizona Walnut is an attractive shade tree. The seeds of *Juglans* do not germinate easily, but once they get started, they have a life expectancy of 300 or 400 years. Some tree trunks have enlarged burls at their bases, suitable for tabletops with beautiful patterns. For irritable bowel syndrome and other chronic colon disorders, a tea of the dried leaves is consumed. Other species of *Juglans* have been used as chewing sticks for cleaning of teeth and gums.
**DESCRIPTION: Height** of this deciduous tree 17 m (57 ft.), usually with a single trunk and widely spreading branches; **bark** of mature trunks dark brown, thick, deeply fissured; **leaves** alternate, odd-pinnately compound, 7 to 11 leaflets per leaf, leaflets lanceolate, serrate, up to 10 cm (4 in.) long; **flowers** (male and female) borne in separate catkins on the same tree; **fruit** is a large, hard-shelled nut surrounded by a husk.

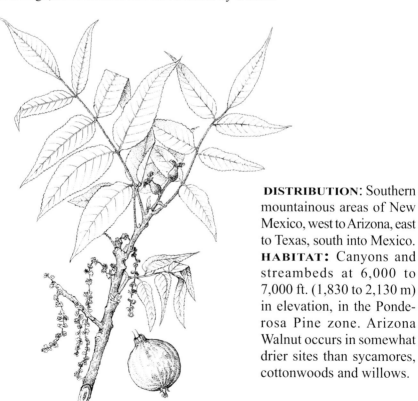

**DISTRIBUTION**: Southern mountainous areas of New Mexico, west to Arizona, east to Texas, south into Mexico. **HABITAT**: Canyons and streambeds at 6,000 to 7,000 ft. (1,830 to 2,130 m) in elevation, in the Ponderosa Pine zone. Arizona Walnut occurs in somewhat drier sites than sycamores, cottonwoods and willows.

## VELVET ASH, ARIZONA ASH
*Fraxinus velutina*
Olive Family (Oleaceae)
**Synonyms:** *Fraxinus pennsylvanica* ssp. *velutina*
*Fraxinus velutina* var. *toumeyi*
**Related Species: Green Ash,** *Fraxinus pennsylvanica*

Velvet Ash is the most common native ash in the southern third of New Mexico. Fast growing and hardy in alkaline soils, it makes a fine shade tree and is planted as an ornamental. Plants can be grown from the seeds, which mature in late summer. The number and shape of leaflets varies considerably in this species. The leaves of Velvet Ash have no mechanisms to prevent water loss, and thus must have access to permanent moisture. Ashes are known for making good firewood; they contain large amounts of oleic acid (a fatty constituent of olive oil), which make the wood flammable.

**DESCRIPTION: Height** of this deciduous tree may reach 12 m (40 ft.); **bark** gray to brown or reddish, with deep fissures, spreading branches forming a rounded crown; **leaves** pinnately compound, leaflets 3 to 7 in number, 3 to 8 cm (1 to 3.5 in.) in length, ovate to elliptic, mostly entire to dentate on the upper half of the leaflet, velvety hairs on the upper leaf surface; **flowers:** male - small and yellow, female - small and green, borne on separate trees and appearing before the leaves in the spring; **fruits** are samaras growing in dense clusters.

**DISTRIBUTION:** Southern third of New Mexico, west to Arizona, Utah, Nevada and California, east to west Texas, and south to Mexico.

**HABITAT:** Canyon bottoms and streambeds at elevations from 4,500 to 8,000 ft. (1,370 to 2,440 m), often found growing with Arizona Walnut.

## ARIZONA SYCAMORE, ARIZONA PLANE-TREE
*Platanus wrightii*
Plane Tree Family (Platanaceae)
**Related Species: American Sycamore,** *Platanus occidentalis*

Arizona Sycamore is a beautiful, distinctive tree, and one finds it in the most enchanting canyons and streambeds. Its mottled bark, spherical hanging fruits, sprawling branches and large, maple-like leaves make it easy to identify. While sycamores generally have a single trunk, sometimes they divide into two or three large trunks near the ground, creating excellent climbing trees for kids. Arizona Sycamore's seeds do not germinate easily, but fortunately they often reproduce vegetatively by sending up suckers from the roots. The eastern related species, American Sycamore, is sometimes planted in lawns, but it requires a tremendous supply of water, which makes it questionable for the Southwest. Red-tailed hawks, mourning doves and many woodpeckers nest in the hollows of sycamores.

**DESCRIPTION: Height** to 25 m (83 ft.) at maturity, trunk diameter larger than 1 m (3 ft.); branches often spreading widely; inner **bark** smooth, white to light green, exposed where older, dark gray bark flakes off; **leaves** alternate, simple, 15 to 25 cm (6 to 10 in.) in width, deeply divided into 5 (sometimes 3 or 7) lobes; **flowers** occur in dense globose heads, with male and female flowers borne separately on the same tree; **fruits** form round heads drooping from long stalks.

**DISTRIBUTION:** Southwest New Mexico, west to Arizona, south into Mexico.

**HABITAT:** Streambeds and canyons at 4,500 to 6,000 ft (1,370 to 1,830 m) in elevation.

# NARROWLEAF COTTONWOOD
*Populus angustifolia*
Willow Family (Salicaceae)

Young Narrowleaf Cottonwoods are often mistaken for willows, because of the similarity in leaf shape. Lewis and Clark, on their historic journey, observed "a species of cottonwood with a leaf like that of the wild cherry." This tree was the Narrowleaf Cottonwood. The pointed, resinous buds of the Narrowleaf Cottonwood distinguish it from the more rounded, resin-less willow buds. And like the willows, Narrowleaf Cottonwood twigs were often woven into baskets by Native Americans. *Populus angustifolia* is fast-growing and suitable for erosion control, but is subject to storm damage. The stems and roots of willows and cottonwoods contain salicylic acid, the active ingredient of aspirin. Beaver eat the bark and can fell young trees. Deer and livestock sometimes browse the young branches. Dyes can be obtained from the spring flowers and summer leaves and twigs. Narrowleaf Cottonwood hybridizes with Fremont Cottonwood (*Populus deltoides*) to produce the Smooth-barked Cottonwood (*Populus X acuminata*). **DESCRIPTION: Height** to 17 m (57 ft.), trunk diameter of up to 0.5 m (20 in.), with a narrow pyramidal crown; **bark** of young trees smooth and light yellow green, becoming thick and fissured into broad, flat ridges; **leaves** alternate, simple, lanceolate to ovate, averaging 5 to 10 cm (2 to 4 in.) in length, with fine teeth on the leaf margins, upper leaf surface bright green to yellow green, lower surface pale green; buds long-pointed and very resinous; **catkins** (male and female) borne on separate trees, appearing before the leaves in the spring; **fruit** a capsule.

**DISTRIBUTION:** Widespread over the western two-thirds of New Mexico, east to western Texas, west to Arizona and California, north to Idaho, Oregon, Montana and Colorado, south to Mexico.
**HABITAT:** Stream sides, in marshy, sandy and gravelly areas at 5,000 to 8,000 ft. (1,520 to 2,440 m) in elevation.

## COTTONWOODS: FREMONT, ALAMO and PLAINS
*Populus deltoides* and *Populus fremontii*
Willow Family (Salicaceae)
**Synonyms:** *Populus wislizeni, Populus sargentii*
**Related Species: Lanceleaf Cottonwood,** *Populus* X *acuminata*

Cottonwoods are planted as ornamentals, grow quickly, and make fine shade trees. (Plant them away from your house: they are subject to storm damage.) Many bird species, including woodpeckers, orioles and owls, nest in cottonwoods. The seeds of cottonwoods lose their viability after only about five weeks, and thus the timing of spring floods is crucial. Seedlings quickly develop long roots that allow them to reach subsurface water after spring floods have receded. Dyes can be obtained from the spring flowers and summer leaves and twigs. The Hopi carve cottonwood roots into kachina dolls, and Pueblo Indians use cottonwood for their drums.

There are two subspecies of *Populus deltoides*: ssp. *wislizeni* and ssp. *monilifera.* There are minor differences in the leaves and leaf stalks, but for our purposes, these two can be considered to be the same. *Populus fremontii* is a Great Basin and Arizona species, and rare in western New Mexico.

**DESCRIPTION: Height** to 30 m (100 ft.), with a wide, open crown, trunk diameter of up to 2 m (6.5 ft.); **bark** rough, thick and furrowed; **leaves** alternate, simple, deltoid or triangular in shape, serrate, leaf blade 5 to 9 cm (2 to 3.5 in.) long, including its long, slender tip, leaf stalk 3 to 5 cm (1 to 2 in.) in length; **flowers** (male and female) borne in catkins on separate trees; **fruit** a capsule containing cottony seeds.

**DISTRIBUTION:** Statewide in New Mexico, north to Colorado, west to Arizona, east to Texas, Oklahoma and Kansas, south to Mexico. The Plains Cottonwood is common throughout much of Eastern North America.

**HABITAT:** Valleys and riverbanks at elevations up to 7,000 ft. (2,130 m).

**CONSERVATION CONSIDERATIONS:** Cottonwood bosques along the Rio Grande and other drainages have been taken over by the invasive tamarisk (salt cedar). Cottonwoods are also susceptible to damage since the young shoots are eaten and trampled by cattle. In many overgrazed southwestern riparian areas, all of the cottonwoods are decades old, with no young trees surviving.

# LANCELEAF COTTONWOOD, SMOOTH-BARKED COTTONWOOD
*Populus* X *acuminata*
Willow Family (Salicaceae)
**Related Species: Plains Cottonwood,** *Populus deltoides* ssp. *monilifera*
**Rio Grande Cottonwood,** *Populus deltoides* ssp.
*wislizeni*

This tree is a hybrid between Narrowleaf Cottonwood (*Populus angustifolia*) and Plains or Rio Grande Cottonwood (*Populus deltoides*). Although some people suffer with hay fever from the cottonwood's "cotton," this tree does have healthful properties. The inner bark of all cottonwoods is edible and can be used to treat Vitamin C deficiencies. The leaves and roots of willows and cottonwoods contain salicylic acid, the active ingredient of aspirin. Beaver eat the bark, and deer and livestock sometimes browse the young branches. The Hopi carve cottonwood roots into kachina dolls. Dyes can be obtained from the spring flowers and summer leaves and twigs.

**DESCRIPTION: Height** to 20 m (67 ft.), with a high, rounded crown; **bark** thick, rough and furrowed; **leaves** alternate, simple, ovate or lanceolate, averaging 4.5 cm (1.75 in.) or more in width, and 6 to 9 cm (2.5 to 3.5 in.) in length, leaf margins serrate; **flowers** male and female catkins borne on separate trees, appearing before the leaves; **fruit** a capsule containing cottony seeds.

**DISTRIBUTION:** Western two-thirds of New Mexico, west to Arizona.

**HABITAT:** Moist or dry soils, on hillsides or in valleys, often in poor soils at 4,500 to 8,000 ft. (1,370 to 2,440 m) in elevation.

## GOODDING'S WILLOW, WESTERN BLACK WILLOW
*Salix gooddingii*
Willow Family (Salicaceae)
**Related Species: Coyote Willow,** *Salix exigua*
**Bluestem Willow,** *Salix irrorata*

Goodding's Willow is a big, beautiful, spreading tree. Its seeds are viable for only nine or ten weeks, so they are completely dependent on the timing and abundance of summer rains. But humans can help in willow reproduction: willows propagate readily by cuttings, and are very useful for reclaiming riparian areas. Goodding's Willow is the Southwest's largest native willow, leading some people to call it "tree willow." As with the other willows and with cottonwoods, the inner bark is edible, and is used to reduce fever, treat arthritis, and cure diarrhea. Beaver eat the bark, and deer and livestock sometimes browse the young branches. Yellow to deep copper dyes can be obtained from the leaves and twigs.

**DESCRIPTION: Height** to 15 m (50 ft.) (occasionally reaching 30 m or 100 ft.) with a trunk diameter of up to 1 m (3 ft.), commonly forked from the base, with two or more widely spreading stems and a broad, loose, irregular crown; younger **twigs** yellowish, older wood dark gray and deeply furrowed; **leaves** alternate, simple, 6.5 to 13 cm (2.5 to 5 in.) in length, 9.5 to 15 mm (about 0.5 in.) in width, leaf margin finely toothed, tip of leaf tapering, lower leaf surface pale green, upper leaf surface bright yellow-green; **flowers** are male and female catkins borne on separate trees; **fruits** are capsules with fine hairs.

**DISTRIBUTION:** Southern and western New Mexico, east to west Texas, west to Arizona and California, south into northern Mexico.

**HABITAT:** Stream sides and arroyos at 4,500 to 7,000 ft. (1,370 to 2,130 m) in elevation.

# WESTERN SOAPBERRY, JABONCILLO
*Sapindus saponaria*
Soapberry Family (Sapindaceae)
**Synonyms:** *Sapindus drummondii*

This attractive tree is often planted as an ornamental. Soapberry has light green leaves, clusters of tiny white flowers, and golden translucent berries that hang from the tree long after the leaves have fallen. *Sapindus* is usually found growing in groves, since it spreads by root sprouts. Its common name derives from the fact that the seeds contain a soaplike substance, saponin, that lathers when placed in water and agitated. Although saponin causes dermatitis in sensitive individuals, the seeds have been used in the southwest U.S. and in Mexico for washing clothes and hair. Native peoples have crushed the seeds and thrown them into streams to stupefy fish. The nectar of the flower is also said to be poisonous. The wood is used for making baskets.

**DESCRIPTION: Height** to 8 to 15 m (25 to 50 ft.); **bark** gray or tan, thin and furrowed; **twigs** yellowish green when young, becoming gray in age; **leaves** alternate, pinnately compound, leaflets 9 to 19, light green on both sides, lanceolate in shape, margins not toothed; **flowers** small and white, borne in dense clusters of male and female panicles on separate trees; **fruit**

a dense cluster of golden-colored, translucent berries each containing 1 or 2 seeds.

**DISTRIBUTION:** Eastern and southern New Mexico, west to Arizona, east to west Texas and the Plains states, north to Colorado, south to Mexico.

**HABITAT:** Moist hillsides, along canyons and ravines, at the margins of wooded areas, from 3,500 to 6,000 ft. (1,070 to 1,830 m) in elevation.

## SMALL TREES OR SHRUBS

Although the words "trees" and "shrubs" are quite familiar, there is some confusion about their meanings. In general, trees are woody plants that have just one main trunk. Shrubs are woody plants with several trunks arising from the base, and typically do not reach the heights of trees.

The plants in this section are often small trees, but in some circumstances will exhibit a more shrubby appearance. To fit your space and needs in gardening, they can be pruned to have only one trunk, and grow into small trees. In their shrubby form, they provide better cover for wildlife and more personal privacy.

"Aspen first captivated me by their visual splendor: the resonance of their autumns, the eloquence of their springs, the opulence of their summers, the elegance of their winters."

Ann Zwinger, *ASPEN, Blazon of the High Country,* 1991

# ROCKY MOUNTAIN MAPLE
*Acer glabrum*
Maple Family (Aceraceae)
**Related Species: Bigtooth Maple,** *Acer grandidentatum*

    Rocky Mountain Maple, the northernmost maple in the New World, is a handsome shrub or small tree with distinctive red leaf stalks. In New Mexico, *Acer glabrum* grows at high elevations. Although it isn't quite as spectacular as its eastern relatives in autumn splendor, its leaves do turn a pale yellow to reddish orange before dropping. Moose, elk and deer browse the foliage, and squirrels and birds eat the seeds.

**DESCRIPTION: Height** of this deciduous shrub or small tree to 7 m (23 ft.), trunk diameter up to 30 cm (1 ft.); **bark** gray to red-brown, smooth or finely fissured; **leaves** opposite, simple or trifoliate, palmately veined, broadly ovate, 2.5 to 6 cm (1 to 2.5 in.) long, and often wider than long, 3 to 5 lobes, sinuses shallow or divided to the midrib, leaf margins toothed, upper leaf surface dark green and lustrous, lower leaf surface paler, leaf stems red; **flowers** greenish yellow, inconspicuous, male and female flowers usually on separate trees but sometimes on the same trees; **fruits** are winged samaras.

**DISTRIBUTION:** Western two thirds of New Mexico, west to Arizona, California, Oregon, Washington, north to Colorado, Canada and Alaska, east to Nebraska and South Dakota.

**HABITAT:** Stream sides and canyons in the foothills, montane and subalpine from 7,000 to 9,500 ft. (2,130 to 2,900 m) in elevation.

# BIGTOOTH MAPLE
*Acer grandidentatum*
Maple Family (Aceraceae)
**Related Species: Rocky Mountain Maple,** *Acer glabrum*

Bigtooth Maple "comes from a good family." Related to the eastern Sugar Maple, its leaves turn red, yellow and orange in the fall. The sap of Bigtooth Maple can be made into syrup, and the hard wood makes excellent fuel. Perhaps its finest use, however, is as a handsome ornamental. The specific name, *grandidentatum*, means "big teeth" and refers to the teeth or lobes of the leaf. Deer browse the leaves.

**DESCRIPTION:** **Height** of tree (sometimes a large shrub) to 15 m (50 ft.); **trunk** to 30 cm (1 ft.) in diameter; **bark** gray to brown, smooth or scaly; **leaves** opposite, thick, 5 to 8 cm (2 to 3.5 in.) long with 3 to 5 lobes, the sinuses between the lobes broad and rounded, upper leaf surface dark green and lustrous, lower leaf paler; **flowers** small, inconspicuous, lacking petals, appearing with the leaves in April to May, growing in the axils; **fruit** a pair of winged samaras, united at the base, 2.5 to 3 cm (1 to 1.25 in.) long.

**DISTRIBUTION:** Southern half of New Mexico, west to Arizona and Utah, north to Colorado, Wyoming, Montana and Idaho, east to Texas and Oklahoma, south to Mexico.

**HABITAT:** Moist canyons, usually growing with coniferous trees, at elevations of 5,500 to 7,500 ft. (1,680 to 2,300 m).

# THINLEAF ALDER, MOUNTAIN ALDER
*Alnus incana* ssp. *tenuifolia*
Birch Family (Betulaceae)
**Synonym:** *Alnus tenuifolia*
**Related Species: New Mexico** or **Arizona Alder**, *Alnus oblongifolia*

Thinleaf Alders are found in nearly impenetrable shrubby stands along mountain streams or in moist meadows. They grow easily and quickly under cultivation, and are attractive shrubs or small trees. The small woody cones remain on the branches throughout the winter, and the seeds attract birds. Beavers, deer and rabbits eat the bark, and many species of birds feed on the seeds. To early settlers, the sight of Thinleaf Alder always meant running water, unlike the cottonwoods which often grow in intermittent waterways. Alders are among the few plants outside of the legume family that are able to fix atmospheric nitrogen. Native Americans used Alder bark to treat burns and other ailments. The bark and twigs can be used to obtain dyes: tan, gold, green and brown. In Mexico, the bark is used for tanning skins.

**DESCRIPTION: Height** of this deciduous large shrub (with stems spreading from the base to form clumps) or small tree to 8 m (25 ft.); **bark** smooth, gray to brown or reddish-brown; **leaves** alternate, simple, ovate to oblong, doubly toothed on the leaf margins, 3 to 11 cm (1 to 4.25 in.) in length and 3 to 6.5 cm (1 to 2.75 in.) in width; **flowers** are catkins, appearing in the spring before the leaves, male and female flowers on separate catkins on the same tree; **fruits** are cones.

**DISTRIBUTION:** Northern New Mexico and southwestern corner of New Mexico, west to Arizona, Utah and California, north to Colorado, western Canada and Alaska, south to Mexico.

**HABITAT:** Stream sides and canyons at 6,500 to 8,500 ft. (1,980 to 2,590 m) in elevation.

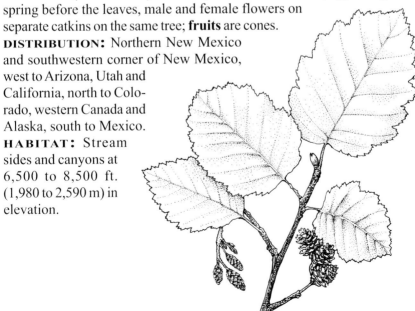

## DESERT WILLOW, MIMBRE
*Chilopsis linearis*
Catalpa Family (Bignoniaceae)

This species is not a willow at all, but its leaves are willow-like in shape; and like willows, it grows in desert washes. Desert Willow is actually a member of the Catalpa family, with the long, slender pods of the catalpas. With its showy, fragrant flowers, Desert Willow is a very attractive shrub or tree and is often planted as an ornamental. It is also important in erosion control. Well adapted to arid environments, *Chilopsis linearis* has low water requirements, and the waxy coating on the leaves prevents water loss. It can be propagated from seeds or cuttings, and grows rapidly. Native Americans used this tree's wood for making bows. The leaves and stems can be powdered or used as a wash to treat skin infections and ringworm, and as a douche for yeast infections. The Mimbres Valley in southwest New Mexico is named for this graceful riparian shrub.

**DESCRIPTION:** **Height** of this deciduous shrub or tree to 10 m (33 ft.), with trunks usually leaning; **bark** smooth and brown on young trees, dark brown to black later; **leaves** simple, alternate or opposite, 7 to 17 cm (3 to 6.75 in.) in length and 5 to 10 mm (0.25 to 0.5 in.) in width, linear to lanceolate, leaf margins entire; **flowers** fragrant and showy, trumpet or bell-shaped, white to purplish red to pink; **fruits** are capsules (although they look like legumes), to 25 cm (10 in.) long, persistent on the branches throughout the winter.

**DISTRIBUTION:** Common over the southern two-thirds of New Mexico, especially along the Rio Grande, west to Arizona, Nevada and California, east to west Texas, south to Mexico.

**HABITAT:** Stream sides and arroyos at 4,000 to 5,500 ft. (1,220 to 1,680 m) in elevation.

## NEW MEXICO ELDER, BLUEBERRY ELDER
*Sambucus cerulea*
Honeysuckle Family (Caprifoliaceae)
**Synonyms:** *S. neomexicana, S. glauca*
**Related Species: Rocky Mountain Elder,** *Sambucus racemosa*
var. *microbotrys*

An attractive shrub or small tree with clusters of fragrant, whitish flowers and bluish fruits, New Mexico Elder is planted as an ornamental. Since it sprouts readily from the base, it is useful for erosion control. Elders are fast growing and can be used as screens or windbreaks. Birds and rodents eat the berries, and humans use them for wines, jellies and pies. The foliage of New Mexico Elder is browsed by deer. Tea made from the bark has been used as a diuretic and purgative, and in cases of difficult childbirth. The straight shoots were used for the shafts of arrows. Whistles and flutes can be fashioned by removing the pith from cut twigs. However, there is some evidence that the stems, roots and leaves are poisonous.

New Mexico Elder looks very similar to Rocky Mountain Elder. It is probably easiest to distinguish the two species by looking at their inflorescenes: flat-topped clusters in New Mexico Elder, and pyramidal in Rocky Mountain Elder. Though their ranges overlap somewhat, Rocky Mountain Elder is found at higher elevations.

**DESCRIPTION: Height** of this deciduous large shrub or small tree to 4 or 5 m (13 to 17 ft.); **bark** brown or gray, furrowed; **leaves** opposite, pinnately compound, 5 to 9 leaflets per leaf, leaflets 9 to 15 cm (3.5 to 6 in.) long, oblong to lanceolate, tapering to a long, thin tip, leaf margins serrate; **flowers** small and cream colored, borne in flat-topped clusters averaging 16

cm (6.5 in.) or more in width; **fruit** a dark blue berry-like drupe, covered with a white waxy coating. **DISTRIBUTION:** Central and southern New Mexico, west to Arizona and California, east to Texas, south to Mexico. **HABITAT:** Stream sides at 7,000 to 9,000 ft. (2,130 to 2,740 m) in elevation, often growing with Ponderosa Pine and Douglas Fir.

## ROCKY MOUNTAIN ELDER
*Sambucus racemosa* var. *microbotrys*
Honeysuckle Family (Caprifoliaceae)
**Synonyms:** *S. melanocarpa, S. pubens*
**Related Species:  New Mexico Elder,** *Sambucus cerulea*

Like its relative New Mexico Elder in the southern part of the state, Rocky Mountain Elder makes an attractive ornamental. It grows quickly, and can be used as a privacy screen or windbreak. The variety name "*microbotrys*" is Greek for a "small bunch of grapes," which the elderberry fruits resemble. The berries can be made into wines, jams and pies.

Rocky Mountain Elder can be distinguished from New Mexico Elder by their flower arrangements: pyramidal in Rocky Mountain Elder, and flat-topped in New Mexico Elder. The berries are red to black in Rocky Mountain Elder, and blue to gray, with a waxy coating, in New Mexico Elder.

**DESCRIPTION: Height** of this deciduous shrub (rarely a small tree) to 3 m (10 ft.); **leaves** opposite, pinnately compound with 5 to 7 leaflets, the leaflets 5 to 15 cm (2 to 6 in.) long, lanceolate to oblong-ovate, leaf margins serrate; **flowers** small, white to pale yellow, in pyramidal clusters that extend above the branches; **fruit** a berry-like drupe, red to black at maturity.

**DISTRIBUTION:** Northern, central and western portions of New Mexico, north to Colorado and Canada, west to California.

**HABITAT:**  Stream banks at 7,000 to 12,000 ft. (2,130 to 3,660 m) in elevation.

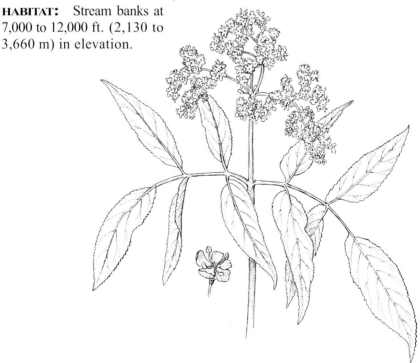

## TEXAS MADRONE, MADROÑO
*Arbutus xalapensis*
Heath Family (Ericaceae)
**Synonym:** *Arbutus texana*
**Related Species: Arizona Madrone**, *Arbutus arizonica*

Texas Madrone is difficult to transplant, but it's worth the effort. Its pinkish bark is very distinctive, peeling off in papery sheets, and becoming dark red in maturity. The flowers of *Madroño*, like those of its relative *Manzanita*, are white to pink and urn-shaped. It tolerates dry soil, must have good drainage, and is not particular about soil type. The wood has been used for fuel, tool handles, and as charcoal for gunpowder. Because of their astringent qualities, the bark and leaves are sometimes used medicinally in Mexico. The fruits are eaten by birds, who are largely responsible for disseminating the seeds.

A closely related species, Arizona Madrone, *Arbutus arizonica,* occurs in Arizona and in extreme southwest New Mexico.

**DESCRIPTION: Height** of this small evergreen tree (occasionally a shrub) to 10 m (33 ft); **bark** thin, pinkish to red-brown, peeling off in large papery sheets; **leaves** leathery, alternate, dark green and smooth on the upper surface, paler below, oblong to obovate, 3 to 8 cm (1 to 3.25 in.) long, 1.8 to 2.5 cm ( to1 in.) wide, leaf margins entire or finely toothed; **flowers** urn-

shaped, white to pink with 5 sepals, 5 petals and 10 stamens; **fruit** berry-like, nearly round, dark red to yellowish-red, waxy.
**DISTRIBUTION:** Southeast corner of New Mexico, east to Texas, south to Mexico.
**HABITAT:** Wooded canyons, mountain slopes and foothill drainages at elevations of 4,000 to 6,500 ft. (1,220 to 1,980 m).

## NEW MEXICO LOCUST
*Robinia neomexicana*
Legume Family (Fabaceae)

New Mexico Locusts, with their beautiful pinkish flowers and attractive foliage, are favorite ornamentals among landscapers. They are fast growing, adaptable to any well drained soil, and have low water requirements. Sprouting freely from stumps and roots, they often form thickets, and are useful for erosion control. They are browsed by deer, chipmunk, mountain sheep and porcupine. The Mescalero and Chiricahua Apaches ate the pods raw or cooked, and considered the flowers to be a great delicacy. Native Americans also used the foliage to treat rheumatism and to induce vomiting. According to Donald Kirk, various writers have reported that the inner bark, roots and seeds may be eaten. But Hardin and Arena, as well as other authors, report that the inner bark, twigs and seeds are poisonous.

**DESCRIPTION: Height** of this deciduous shrub or small tree to 8 m (25 ft.); **leaves** alternate, compound, 9 to 23 leaflets per leaf, leaflets elliptic, margins entire, a pair of sharp, stout spines at the base of each leaf; **flowers** are showy, pea-like, petals rose to bluish-purple, borne in many-flowered racemes; **fruits** are hairy pods to 10 cm (4 in.) long.

**DISTRIBUTION:** Common over much of New Mexico, east to western Texas, west to Arizona, north to Colorado, Utah and Nevada, south to Mexico.

**HABITAT:** River bottoms, stream banks and north-facing canyon slopes at 4,500 to 9,000 ft. (1,370 to 2,740 m) in elevation. Often found growing with Gambel Oak, *Quercus gambelii*.

## EMORY OAK
*Quercus emoryi*
Oak Family (Fagaceae)
**Related Species: Gray Oak,** *Quercus grisea*

Emory Oak keeps its leaves throughout the cold months, lending some green to the southwestern winter landscape. In the spring, it drops its leaves, and new leaves grow when there is sufficient moisture. The specific name, *emoryi*, honors First Lieutenant William Helmsly Emory, of the U. S. Army Topographic Corps who served in the Army of the West under General Stephen W. Kearny in 1846. Emory Pass in the Black Range is also named for Lt. Emory. The leaves of Emory Oak are heavily browsed by mule deer, and the acorns are eaten by birds, chipmunks and squirrels. In addition, the acorns were gathered and eaten by Native Americans and Mexican-Americans. Although Native Americans still gather Emory Oak acorns, legend has it that they will not gather them in Cochise's stronghold, out of reverence for the Apache leader and his burial ground.

**DESCRIPTION: Height** of this shrub or tree to 20 m (67 ft.); **bark** dark brown or black, old trunks fissured; **leaves** alternate, simple, persistent through winter, thick and leathery, lanceolate to oblong, shiny on both upper and lower surfaces, 2 to 7.5 cm (0.75 to 3 in.) in length and 0.8 to 3 cm (0.25 to 1 in.) in width, coarsely 2 to 4 toothed on each margin or entire; **flowers** are small, yellow and inconspicuous, male and female catkins appearing on the same tree; **fruits** are acorns, dark brown to black at maturity.

**DISTRIBUTION:** Southwestern portion of New Mexico, west to Arizona, east to west Texas, south to Mexico.

**HABITAT:** Plains and piñon-juniper and oak woodlands at 4,000 to 6,500 ft. (1,220 to 1,980 m) in elevation.

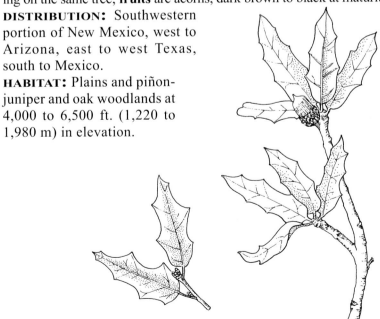

## GAMBEL OAK
*Quercus gambelii*
Oak Family (Fagaceae)

Gambel Oak is the southwest's only native oak that loses its leaves in the fall. It is also the only oak in the southwest with the deeply lobed leaves usually associated with eastern oaks. A slow-growing tree, Gambel Oak's leaves turn yellow and sometimes red before they fall in autumn. *Quercus gambelii* spreads by root sprouts, and forms colonies. Its acorns can be eaten directly from the tree, whereas acorns of most other oaks need to be soaked to leach out the tannic acid. Dried acorns can be made into meal, then used to make mush, soup, bread and pancakes. Native Americans used powdered bark to treat skin sores and skin cancer, gum inflammations, and abrasions. A tea from the bark was used in the treatment of diarrhea and malaria. Deer and porcupine browse the foliage, wild turkey and squirrels eat the acorns, and the tree provides cover for wildlife.

**DESCRIPTION:** **Height** of this deciduous shrub or small tree to 15 m (50 ft.); **bark** gray and rough; **leaves** alternate, simple, 5 to 15 cm (2 to 6 in.) in length, with 5 to 9 distinct, deeply divided (more than halfway to the midvein) lobes, upper leaf surface smooth and shiny green, lower leaf surface duller and hairy; **flowers** are inconspicuous, male and female catkins appearing on the same tree; **fruit** an acorn 8 to 20 mm (to 0.75 in.) in length, borne singly or in clusters of 2 or 3.

**DISTRIBUTION:** Widely scattered over New Mexico, west to Arizona and Nevada, north to Colorado and Wyoming, east to Texas and Oklahoma, south to northern Mexico.

**HABITAT:** Canyons, stream sides, and in dry montane forests with ponderosa pines, at elevations of 6,000 to 8,500 ft. (1,830 to 2,590 m).

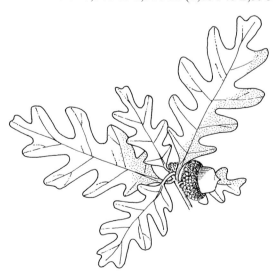

## GRAY OAK, SCRUB OAK
*Quercus grisea*
Oak Family (Fagaceae)
**Related Species: Emory Oak,** *Quercus emoryi*

The leaves of Gray Oak are highly variable: even on the same tree, you may find different shapes, sizes, and margins. *Quercus grisea* can be difficult to distinguish from Emory Oak (*Q. emoryi*), with which it often grows. The leaves of Gray Oak are a dull gray-green in color, and Emory Oak's leaves are a glossy green on the upper surface. Gray Oak sometimes hybridizes with Arizona White Oak (*Q. arizonica*), Scrub Live Oak (*Q. turbinella*), and others, again causing confusion. Gray Oak's foliage is browsed by deer and porcupines, and squirrels feed on the acorns. Since oaks contain tannic acid, the acorns must first be soaked, and then they can be made into flour and used in soups, breads, and other foods.

**DESCRIPTION: Height** of this shrub or tree ranging from 1 to 10 m (3 to 33 ft.); **bark** is dark gray with ridges and furrows; **leaves** alternate, simple, persistent through winter, thick and leathery, 3 cm (1.25 in.) or more in length, dull gray-green in color, oblong to elliptic or ovate, upper and lower leaf surfaces hairy, leaf margins usually entire, but sometimes toothed; **flowers** are inconspicuous catkins, male and female catkins borne on the same tree; **fruits** are acorns borne singly or in pairs.

**DISTRIBUTION:** Widespread over most of New Mexico, west to Arizona, east to western Texas, south to Mexico.

**HABITAT:** Forests, woodland and savannas at 4,700 to 7,200 ft. (1,430 to 2,200 m) in elevation.

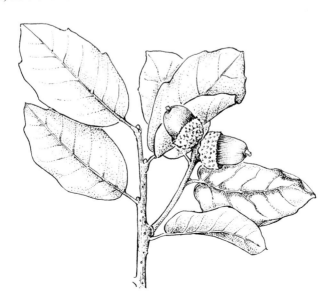

## LITTLE WALNUT
*Juglans microcarpa*
Walnut Family (Juglandaceae)
**Related Species: Arizona Walnut,** *Juglans major*

Little Walnut, an attractive shrub or small tree, is an ideal plant for a limited growing space. This species is very similar to Arizona Walnut. The two can be distinguished by growth habit: Little Walnut is a shrub or small tree, while Arizona Walnut can grow to 17 m (57 ft.) in height. Also, the number of leaflets distinguishes them: Little Walnut has 15 to 23 leaflets per leaf, and Arizona Walnut has 9 to 13. The walnuts of *Juglans microcarpa,* smaller than those of Arizona Walnut, are eaten by squirrels and other rodents, and wildlife use it for cover. Other species in the genus *Juglans* have been used for chewing sticks to clean teeth and gums, and for decoctions to treat skin diseases.

**DESCRIPTION: Height** of this deciduous shrub or tree to 6 m (20 ft.), often with a number of leaning trunks from the base; **bark** brown, deeply fissured; **leaves** alternate, pinnately compound, 15 to 23 leaflets per leaf, leaflets ovate to lanceolate, 3 to 9 cm (1 to 3.5 in.) long, leaflet margins serrate, upper leaf surface dark yellow-green, lower leaf surface slightly paler; **flowers** are male and female catkins borne on the same tree; **fruits** are nuts to 2 cm (0.75 in.) in diameter, borne singly or 2 to 3 in a cluster.

**DISTRIBUTION:** Southern New Mexico, east to Texas, Oklahoma and Kansas, south to northern Mexico.

**HABITAT:** Canyons and stream sides, dry ravine banks and hillsides, at elevations of 3,500 to 6,000 ft. (1,070 to 1,830 m).

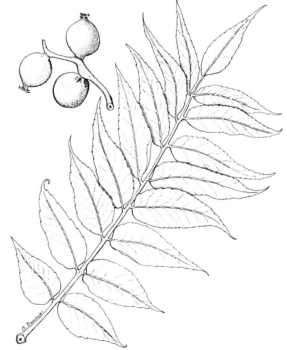

## WESTERN or **COMMON CHOKECHERRY** and **SOUTHWESTERN CHOKECHERRY**
*Prunus virginiana* and *Prunus serotina*
Rose Family (Rosaceae)

Attractive plants, especially when in flower and fruit, Chokecherries are planted as ornamentals. The bitter taste of the fruits gave rise to the name "chokecherry." Given enough sweetener, the fruits can be made into jellies, syrups, juices and wines. The Navajo considered *Prunus* to be sacred, and used its wood for prayersticks. Plains Indians, too, held them in high esteem, and the whole community was involved in gathering the fruit. Native Americans and early settlers used the root to treat malaria, worms, tuberculosis, indigestion and fever. Dyes of earth tones can be obtained from the twigs and leaves, and pinkish tan to gray-green dyes from the cherries. Many species in the genus *Prunus* have toxic amounts of cyanide in their leaves and in the cherry pits, and caution is advised.

**DESCRIPTION: Height** of this deciduous shrub or small tree to 8 m (25 ft.); **bark** on young trees red brown and smooth, becoming gray and slightly furrowed with age; **leaves** alternate, simple, ovate to elliptic or obovate, abruptly acute at the apex, 4 to 12 cm (1.5 to 5 in.) in length, dark green and somewhat lustrous on the upper leaf surface, grayish green on lower leaf surface, leaf margins finely toothed; **flowers** white, in dense clusters, 7 to 15 cm (3 to 6 in.) in length; **fruits** are fleshy, round, purple-black berry-like drupes, growing in long spikes. Southwestern Chokecherry is difficult to distinguish from Western Chokecherry, and their habitats and ranges overlap in southern New Mexico. Probably the easiest way to tell these two species apart is by examining them in fruit. Southwestern Chokecherry fruit will usually

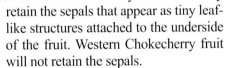

retain the sepals that appear as tiny leaf-like structures attached to the underside of the fruit. Western Chokecherry fruit will not retain the sepals.

**DISTRIBUTION:** Western Chokecherry is widespread throughout New Mexico, west to Arizona, California, Oregon and Washington, east to Texas, Kansas, Missouri, Tennessee and North Carolina, north to Colorado and Canada. Southwestern Chokecherry is restricted to southern New Mexico, west Texas, Arizona, and Mexico.

**HABITAT:** Moist canyons and along streams at elevations of 4,500 to 8,000 ft. (1,370 to 2,440 m).

116

## HOP TREE, WAFER ASH
*Ptelea trifoliata*
Citrus Family (Rutaceae)
**Synonyms**: *Ptelea angustifolia, Ptelea pallida*

Hop Tree is fairly easy to identify: just look for three leaflets and the fruits: two or three seeds surrounded by a thin, papery, round wing. This plant can be grown as a shrub or pruned into a small tree. Its fragrant, greenish white flower clusters appear in early summer. *Ptelea trifoliata* tolerates poor, rocky soil and has low water requirements. If you crumble the leaves of Hop Tree, you will smell the strong odor of citric acid (this species is in the same family with citrus fruits). The fruits have been used as a substitute for hops in brewing beer. They can also be mixed with yeast to make an exceptionally light loaf of bread. The roots have medicinal qualities, having been substituted for quinine in combating malaria. Native Americans also considered the bark to be a sacred medicine.

**DESCRIPTION: Height** of this deciduous shrub or small tree to 6 m (20 ft.); **bark** red brown and smooth, becoming slightly fissured with age; **leaves** alternate, compound, three leaflets per leaf, lustrous, dark green, leaf margin entire or finely toothed; **flowers** small, green to white in color and growing in dense clusters, unisexual and bisexual flowers on the same plant; **fruit** is a dry, straw-colored, round, flattened samara, with a thin wing surrounding the seeds, 1 to 2 cm (0.5 to 1 in.) in diameter, growing in drooping clusters.

**DISTRIBUTION:** Southern two-thirds of New Mexico, west to Arizona and California, north to Colorado, east to Texas, the Plains states and the southeastern US, south to Mexico.

**HABITAT:** Canyons and rocky areas at elevations of 4,000 to 8,000 ft. (1,220 to 2,440 m).

# QUAKING ASPEN
*Populus tremuloides*
Willow Family (Salicaceae)

Quaking Aspen receives its common name from its leaves which, because of their long flattened leaf stalks, tremble in the slightest breeze. André Michaux, a French botanist of the 17th century, gave the specific name, *tremuloides,* because French woodcutters called them "quakies." Aspens, one of the most widely distributed trees in North America, are easy to distinguish from other trees because of their smooth white bark, often slashed by bears' claws, and by their lustrous green foliage. Aspen seeds are light and cottony, and easily borne by the wind; this may account for their widespread occurrence. But because aspen seeds are short-lived, most aspens spread by root sprouts forming clones. They are pioneer trees in burned areas, rapidly forming thickets, and are later replaced by conifers. It is a quick-growing species, intolerant of shade, and lives to about 100 years old. Deer and elk use aspens for cover and feed on tender shoots. Beavers use the trees for both food and dam construction materials. Bees visit the flowers for food, and many birds eat the seeds. Quaking Aspen groves turn a brilliant golden color in autumn, and stand out in contrast against the green mountainsides. Twigs and green leaves produce dyes of the following colors: yellow, brown, gold and olive green.

**DESCRIPTION: Height** of this deciduous tree to 20 m (40 to 67 ft.); **bark** smooth, gray or greenish white, marked with dark, raised, eye-shaped branch scars; **leaves** alternate, simple, broadly ovate to almost orbicular, 3 to 8 cm (1 to 3.5 in.) in diameter, leaf margins finely toothed, upper leaf surface bright, lustrous green, lower leaf surface duller green, leaf stalk to 6 cm (2.5 in.) long; **inflorescences** are drooping, many-flowered male and female catkins appearing on separate trees; **fruit** is a capsule 5 to 7 mm (0.25 in.) long.

**DISTRIBUTION:** Widespread over New Mexico, west to Arizona and California, north to Colorado and Canada, east to Texas, south to Mexico.

**HABITAT:** Mountainous areas, on slopes and in valleys at elevations of 6,500 to 10,500 ft. (1,980 to 3,200 m).

## NETLEAF HACKBERRY, PALO BLANCO
*Celtis reticulata*
Elm Family (Ulmaceae)
**Synonyms:** *Celtis laevigata* var. *reticulata*
                 *Celtis douglasii*

    The Spanish common name of this species, *Palo Blanco* (White Wood), refers to its sapwood, which is very light in color. Netleaf Hackberry has a strong taproot, but also many shallow roots, making it good for erosion control. It can live up to 200 years, and can withstand drought and high temperatures. Netleaf Hackberry provides cover for wildlife and nesting sites for doves and desert songbirds. Squirrels and birds consume the fruits, which persist through the winter when there is often little else to eat. Two species of butterflies rely on the foliage of Hackberry for caterpillar food. The small orange or yellow fruits are edible raw, and are somewhat sweet. Native Americans used the fruits' seeds and flesh to pound into a pulp; the mashed fruits were then eaten with fat or mixed with parched corn.

**DESCRIPTION: Height** of this deciduous shrub or tree to 8 m (26 ft.), the limbs usually crooked; **bark** pale gray and thin, smooth or cracked, becoming warty on old trees; **leaves** alternate, simple, ovate to lanceolate, 3 to 6.5 cm (1 to 2.75 in.) in length and 2 to 4.5 cm (0.75 to 1.75 in.) in width, leaf margins mostly entire or occasionally somewhat serrate above the middle, prominently reticulate veined on the lower surface, leaf bases asymmetrical, leaf surfaces rough and sandpapery; **flowers** small and inconspicuous, both male and female flowers borne on the same tree; **fruit** an orbicular drupe, red to orange to brown.

**DISTRIBUTION:** Widespread in New Mexico, west to Arizona, east to Texas, Nebraska and Kansas, south to Mexico.
**HABITAT:** Dry rocky hillsides and ravine banks at 3,500 to 6,000 ft. (1,070 to 1,830 m) in elevation.

# SHRUBS

In the arid Southwest, many wildflowers complete their entire life cycles during the rainy season. Desert shrubs do not have this luxury. They have evolved strategies for surviving the hottest, driest, harshest times of year, as well as during the "monsoons."

This book includes shrubs of higher elevations, as well as of the desert. Uplands shrubs have adapted to lower temperatures by losing their leaves and going dormant in the winter. While many of the species in this section are deciduous, lack of leaves and flowers won't leave your garden looking drab in winter. Many of the plants in this section retain their fruits all winter, and some have beautiful bark that becomes more conspicuous in winter.

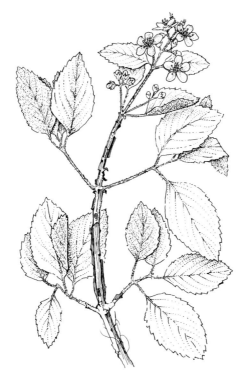

"The people of the European race in coming into the New World have not really sought to make friends of the native population, or to make adequate use of the plants or the animals indigenous to this continent, but rather to exterminate everything found here and to supplant it with the plants and animals to which they are accustomed at home."
Melvin Gilmore, *Uses of Plants by the Indians of the Missouri River Region* (1919)
from *Prairy Erth* by William Least Heat-Moon

## DESERT HONEYSUCKLE, CHUPAROSA
*Anisacanthus thurberi*
Acanthus Family (Acanthaceae)

   Desert Honeysuckle is an excellent addition to a low elevation hummingbird garden, because hummers love its orange-red flowers and abundant nectar. It is visited by other pollinators as well: solitary bees and other insects can see its orange color (many insects do not see red) and can reach the nectar in the short floral tube. Many desert shrubs lose their leaves when there is insufficient moisture, but Desert Honeysuckle only drops its leaves after the first hard frost.

**DESCRIPTION: Height** of this deciduous shrub to 2.5 m (8 ft.); older branches whitish, shredding into fibrous strips; **leaves** in whorls around the branches, lanceolate to elliptic to oblong, leaf margins entire, leaf surfaces a dull olive green, leaf blades to 5 cm (2 in.) long; **flowers** showy, tubular, orange-red to red (sometimes white), borne singly in the leaf axils; **fruit** a capsule.

**DISTRIBUTION:** Southwest corner of New Mexico, west to Arizona, south to Mexico.

**HABITAT:** Dry rocky mesas, canyons and arroyos at 4,000 to 5,500 ft. (1,220 to 1,680 m) in elevation.

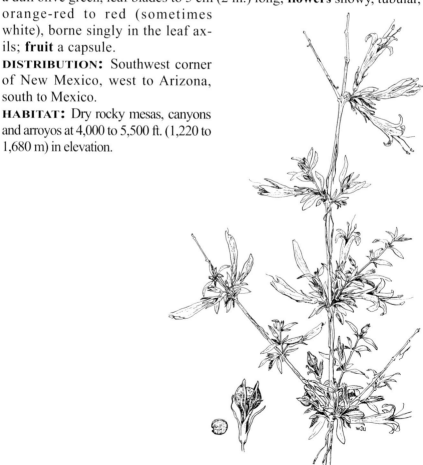

## SKUNKBUSH, THREE LEAF SUMAC
*Rhus trilobata*
Sumac Family (Anacardiaceae)
**Synonym:** *Rhus aromatica*
**Related Species: Smooth Sumac,** *Rhus glabra*

If browsing animals are a concern, this shrub is a good choice because nothing eats Skunkbush! It does provide good cover for small mammals and birds. The red fruits can be made into a refreshing drink with a tart, lemony flavor, and so this plant is sometimes called "lemonade berry." Pop a few berries into your mouth on a hot day, and they will help to alleviate your thirst by stimulating the flow of saliva. Native Americans dried these berries for future use, and they went into the making of pemmican. The common name "Squawbush" arose because Native American women used the flexible young stems for weaving baskets, and the twigs supplied a yellow dye. The leaves of Skunkbush turn a rich red or orange color before they drop in the fall.

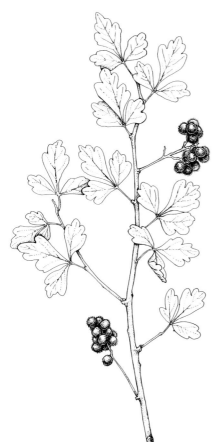

**DESCRIPTION: Height** of this deciduous shrub to 2 m (6.5 ft.) with several trunks from the base; **twigs** velvety hairy when young; **leaves** alternate, compound, tri-foliate, leaflets 1 to 3.5 cm (0.5 to 1.5 in.) in length, leaflet surfaces often pubescent, leaflets lanceolate to ovate to elliptic in outline, leaflet margins lobed or coarsely toothed; **flowers** small, yellow, borne in small tight clusters in the early spring, both male and female reproductive organs together in one flower; **fruit** a drupe, red to orange, hairy and sticky, borne in dense clusters.

**DISTRIBUTION:** Widespread over New Mexico, west to Arizona and California, north to Colorado, east to Texas, south to Mexico.

**HABITAT:** Woods, hills, rocky soils at 5,000 to 7,500 ft. (1,520 to 2,300 m) in elevation.

## SMOOTH SUMAC, SCARLET SUMAC
*Rhus glabra*
Sumac Family (Anacardiaceae)
**Related Species: Three Leaf Sumac**, *Rhus aromatica*

In the fall, Smooth Sumac really catches the eye with its scarlet foliage. This shrub often grows in thickets, and an entire hillside turns red. Smooth Sumac provides cover for rabbits, chipmunks and other small animals, and the berries provide food for mammals and many species of birds. A lemonade-like drink can be made from the berries. Smooth Sumac has many medicinal uses. In Appalachia, the leaves were rolled and smoked to treat asthma. The fruits can be used as a gargle to relieve sore throats. The bark, boiled in milk, is a treatment for burns. A decoction of bark from the stem or roots is used to treat skin ulcers, gonorrhea, diarrhea and infected lymph glands. Smooth Sumac is shallowly rooted and transplants easily.

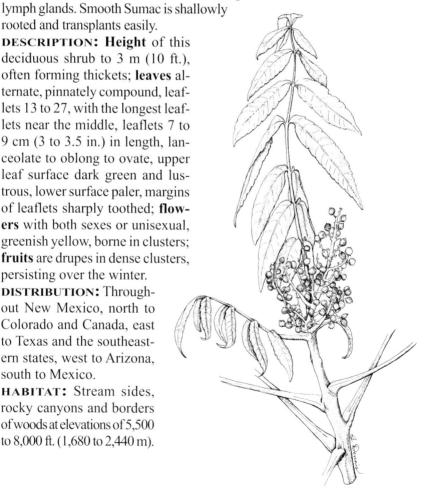

**DESCRIPTION: Height** of this deciduous shrub to 3 m (10 ft.), often forming thickets; **leaves** alternate, pinnately compound, leaflets 13 to 27, with the longest leaflets near the middle, leaflets 7 to 9 cm (3 to 3.5 in.) in length, lanceolate to oblong to ovate, upper leaf surface dark green and lustrous, lower surface paler, margins of leaflets sharply toothed; **flowers** with both sexes or unisexual, greenish yellow, borne in clusters; **fruits** are drupes in dense clusters, persisting over the winter.

**DISTRIBUTION:** Throughout New Mexico, north to Colorado and Canada, east to Texas and the southeastern states, west to Arizona, south to Mexico.

**HABITAT:** Stream sides, rocky canyons and borders of woods at elevations of 5,500 to 8,000 ft. (1,680 to 2,440 m).

## PASTURE SAGE, ESTAFIATA
*Artemisia frigida*
Composite Family (Asteraceae)
**Related Species: Big Sagebrush,** *Artemisia tridentata*

Pasture Sage, with its tall flower spikes and aromatic foliage, makes an interesting autumn accent plant. Plains Indians had many medicinal uses for this common sage, which they called "she sage." The Hopi roasted leaves of Pasture Sage with corn to add flavoring. This species is a source of camphor, and its leaves can be chewed as a treatment for heartburn and applied to reduce swelling and nosebleed. A tea from the leaves is used in treatment of colds and sore eyes and as a hair tonic. The pollen is a source of hay fever, and is also used in remedial extracts. Pasture Sage is winter-grazed by elk and bighorn sheep. Dyes of light yellow to dark green can be obtained from the new stalks and leaves.

**DESCRIPTION: Height** of this shrub to 50 cm (1.5 ft.) at maturity, branched from the base; taller stems silky-hairy, becoming somewhat woody with age, and extending separately above the basal cluster of leaves; **leaves** mostly found at the base of the plant, 20 cm (8 in.) or less above the soil level, often reclining or forming woody mats, leaves alternate, simple, about 1 cm (0.5 in.) in length, deeply divided or dissected to the midrib, leaf segments linear to oblong, leaf surfaces white-hairy with an aroma of sage; **flowers** in heads borne in narrow spikes, appearing in late summer and fall; **fruit** is an achene.

**DISTRIBUTION:** Northern two-thirds of New Mexico, west to Arizona and Utah, north to Colorado, North and South Dakota, and Canada, east to west Texas and Nebraska.

**HABITAT:** Dry soils at 5,500 to 8,000 ft. (1,680 to 2,440 m) in elevation.

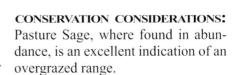

**CONSERVATION CONSIDERATIONS:** Pasture Sage, where found in abundance, is an excellent indication of an overgrazed range.

## BIG SAGEBRUSH
*Artemisia tridentata*
Composite Family (Asteraceae)
**Related Species: Pasture Sage,** *Artemisia frigida*

This is the most widely distributed shrub of the Western United States; in some areas it may be the only plant in sight. Big Sagebrush is known to cause hay fever, and an extract of the plant is used in its treatment. The leaves can be made into a tea and used for treating a wide variety of ailments. According to herbalist Michael Moore, *Artemisia tridentata* is the most useful and worst tasting of the *Artemisias,* and any teas should be sipped slowly, before the gag reflex sets in. A wash made of boiled leaves was used for treating bullet wounds and cuts. The seeds and fruits may be dried, pounded into meal to make *pinole* (flour), or eaten raw. This species is eaten by many birds and mammals. The fragrance of Big Sagebrush is due to chemicals called terpenoids found in the leaf hairs. Terpenoids act as natural insecticides to deter caterpillars and grasshoppers. The hairs on the plants reflect excess sunlight, and help to prevent water loss and keep the plant cool. Dyes of bright colors, such as gold and rust, can be obtained from the plant in late summer.

**DESCRIPTION: Height** of this shrub 3 to 4 m (10 to 13 ft.) at maturity; **twigs** white woolly; **leaves** alternate, simple, 0.5 to 5 cm (to 2 in.) long, leaf tip 3-lobed or sometimes 5-lobed, some of the upper leaves entire, leaf surfaces silvery-hairy, leaves wedge-shaped, many leaves persistent through winter; **flowers** are pale yellow, growing in heads borne in spikes; **fruit** is an achene.

**DISTRIBUTION:** Northern and especially the northwestern portion of New Mexico, west to Arizona and California, north to Colorado, Montana, Wyoming, Washington and Canada, east to Texas, south to northern Mexico.

**HABITAT:** Dry plains and mesas, rocky slopes at elevations of 4,500 to 8,500 ft. (1,370 to 2,590 m).

**CONSERVATION CONSIDERATIONS:** Big Sagebrush is often found in solid stands where overgrazing has occurred.

## SEEPWILLOW BACCHARIS
*Baccharis salicifolia*
Composite Family (Asteraceae)
**Synonym:** *Baccharis glutinosa*

Seepwillow Baccharis, a very common riparian plant throughout the Southwest, is not a willow at all, despite its common name, but the two species can often be found growing together. With its graceful willow-like leaves and long flowering season, Seepwillow is an attractive ornamental. Its leaves have a distinctive aroma, which, once learned, can help you with identification. Seepwillow Baccharis grows quickly and can form thickets, making it useful for erosion control and riparian restoration. This shrub sometimes functions as a "nursery" plant, shielding young cottonwoods and willows from predators and sunlight. Seepwillow Baccharis is visited by bees, wasps, and many species of butterfly. Called *Yerba del Pasmo* by herbalists, all species of the genus *Baccharis* are used medicinally. A tea from the leaves is used to treat hay fever and sinusitis, and can be used as a wash to clean and dress wounds.

**DESCRIPTION: Height** of this deciduous shrub 1 to 3.5 m (3 to 11.5 ft.),

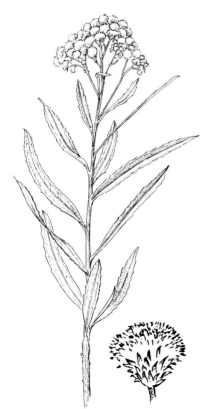

woody only at the base, many un-branched stems arising from the base; **leaves** alternate, simple, resinous, dark, shiny green, linear to lanceolate, 5 to 12 cm (2 to 5 in.) in length and 4 to 18 mm (to 0.8 in.) in width, conspicuously 3-nerved, leaf margin coarsely toothed to entire; **flowers** cream colored or yel-low, ray flowers absent, in large, round clusters of small heads at the ends of the branches, male and female flowers borne on separate plants; **fruit** an achene with a silky tail.

**DISTRIBUTION:** Common over much of New Mexico, west to Arizona, Ne-vada, Utah and California, north to Colorado, east to Texas, south to Mexico.

**HABITAT:** Low moist areas, adjacent to streams and ponds at 3,500 to 5,000 ft. (1,070 to 1,520 m) in elevation.

## BRICKELLBUSH, TASSELFLOWER
*Brickellia grandiflora*
Composite Family (Asteraceae)

This handsome shrub is sometimes called Tasselflower, because its flower heads resemble tassels, especially after they have gone to seed. There are many species in the genus *Brickellia*, and *B. grandiflora* is one of the most common. Brickellbush grows in a wide variety of habitats and elevations. It flowers in the late summer and fall, like many members of the Asteraceae family. For treating adult-onset, insulin-resistant diabetes, herbalists recommend a strong cup of Brickellbush tea taken twice daily. The stems of this plant yield dyes ranging in color from light yellow to golden brown.

**DESCRIPTION: Height** of this small, deciduous shrub to 1 m (3 ft.), woody only at the base; **leaves** alternate, simple, thin, lanceolate with a long tapering tip, dark green in color, 2.5 to 10 cm (1 to 4 in.) in length and 1.5 to 8 cm (0.75 to 3.25 in.) in width, leaf margins coarsely toothed; **flowers** cream-colored, 20 to 40 small flowers per head, usually nodding, ray flowers absent; **fruit** an achene.

**DISTRIBUTION:** This common shrub is found throughout the western two-thirds of New Mexico, west to Arizona and California, north to Colorado, south to Mexico.

**HABITAT:** Canyons and rocky slopes at 4,500 to 10,000 ft. (1,370 to 3,050 m) in elevation, from piñon-juniper to pine, spruce and fir forests.

# TURPENTINE BUSH
*Ericameria laricifolia*
Composite Family (Asteraceae)
**Synonym:** *Haplopappus laricifolius*
**Related Species: Rabbitbrush,** *Ericameria nauseosa*

In the fall, this compact green shrub is stunning with its dark green foliage and crown of bright yellow flowers. When in bloom, you can see that Turpentine Bush is in the same genus (*Ericameria*) as Rabbitbrush. They are both late bloomers with eye-catching flowers. Crush the leaves, and you'll know why this plant is called Turpentine Bush. Its strong but pleasing smell helps in identification. *Ericameria laricifolia* has low water requirements. Its sap contains small amounts of rubber.

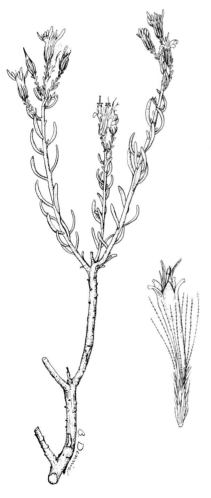

**DESCRIPTION: Height** of this evergreen shrub to 1 m (3 ft.) or more at maturity; **leaves** small, densely crowded, grayish-green to bright green, linear or needle-shaped, rigid, covered with many resinous glands, sticky, exuding a strong turpentine-like odor; **flowers** small, bright yellow, borne in heads; **fruit** an achene.

**DISTRIBUTION:** Southern and southwestern New Mexico, west to Arizona, east to Texas, south to Mexico.

**HABITAT:** Dry hills and rocky canyons at elevations of 3,500 to 6,000 ft. (1,070 to 1,830 m).

## RABBITBRUSH, CHAMISA
*Ericameria nauseosa*
Composite Family (Asteraceae)
**Synonym:** *Chrysothamnus nauseosus*
**Related Species: Turpentine Bush,** *Ericameria laricifolia*

When you see Rabbitbrush in bloom, with its numerous bright yellow flowers, you know autumn is at hand. Because it blooms late in the season when most flowers have already gone to seed, Rabbitbrush is visited heavily by bees, wasps and butterflies. The foliage and seeds are eaten by rabbits and other mammals. This is a very diverse species, and many authorities have divided it into numerous subspecies and varieties. Rabbitbrush, because it tolerates poor soils, is useful for reclaiming disturbed areas and for controlling erosion. The flowers yield a yellow dye used by the Navajo, and the inner bark can be used for a green dye. Depending on when the plant is harvested, the stems and leaves can also yield dyes of gold, rust and orange colors. The Hopi use the wood for kiva fuels, basket making and windbreaks. A tea is taken to break fevers and promote sweating, and the plant's latex has been used for chewing gum.

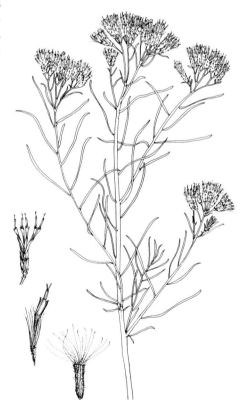

**DESCRIPTION: Height** of this shrub to 3 m (10 ft.), bearing several erect stems from the base to form a rounded clump; **twigs** densely woolly; **leaves** alternate, simple, lacking a leaf stem, linear in shape, woolly, 2 to 8 cm (to 3.5 in.) in length,1- to 3-nerved; **flowers** yellow, feathery, in flat-topped or rounded heads at the tips of the branches, flowering in late summer and fall; **fruit** an achene.

**DISTRIBUTION:** Widespread throughout New Mexico, west to Arizona and California, north to Colorado, Washington and Canada, east to Texas and the Dakotas, south into Mexico.

**HABITAT:** Dry plains and hills to dry streambeds and stream margins at 4,000 to 8,000 ft. (1,220 to 2,440 m) in elevation.

## DOUGLAS GROUNDSEL
*Senecio flaccidus* var. *douglasii*
Composite Family (Asteraceae)
**Synonym:** *Senecio douglasii* ssp. *longilobus*

Douglas Groundsel's grayish-green foliage and bright yellow flowers make it a good choice for an accent plant. It blooms all season long - April through October - and grows in a wide variety of habitats and elevations. Douglas Groundsel increases rapidly in disturbed and overgrazed areas. Nevertheless, it is an attractive native plant and has potential as an ornamental. The genus name, *Senecio*, comes from the Latin *senex*, for "old man," and refers to the white hairs of many species. Although *Senecios* have reportedly been used medicinally, they contain liver toxins, are poisonous to humans and cattle and should not be ingested.

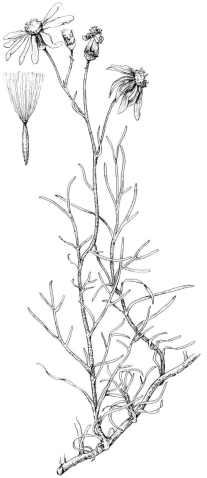

**DESCRIPTION: Height** of this shrub, woody only at the base, from 80 to 130 cm (3 to 4.5 ft.) at maturity; **leaves** alternate, grayish-green, linear, densely hairy (smooth in some varieties), some leaves divided into narrow linear segments, some leaves not divided; **flowers** yellow, with 8 to 17 rays in a head, the flower heads extending above the leaves; **fruit** an achene.

**DISTRIBUTION:** Southern half of New Mexico, north to Colorado, west to Arizona and Utah, east to Texas, south to Mexico.

**HABITAT:** Wide range of habitats, including sandy and rocky soils, on the plains, in washes and disturbed areas, at elevations of 3,000 to 8,000 ft. (910 to 2,440 m).

## ALGERITA, RED OREGON-GRAPE
*Berberis haematocarpa*
Barberry Family (Berberidaceae)
**Synonym:** *Mahonia haematocarpa*
**Related Species: Desert Oregon-Grape,** *Berberis fremontii*
            **Creeping Oregon-Grape***, Berberis repens*

Red Oregon-Grape, with its evergreen leaves, fragrant yellow flowers and bright red berries, is an attractive plant for cultivation. *Berberis* can tolerate drought, heat and sun. The fruits are used in making jam, but you'll have to beat the birds to them. Gambel's Quail and other ground feeding birds are attracted to the berries. Butterflies and bees visit the flowers, and the plant is used for cover by many small animals. The root and bark can be made into a yellow dye, and the fruits produce purple and lavender dyes.

Desert Oregon-Grape is very similar to Red Oregon-Grape. Its mature berries are purple to blue-black, rather than red. Also, its leaves have a shorter, broader appearance than the leaflets of Red Oregon-Grape. *Berberis fremontii* and *B. haematocarpa* occupy much the same habitat and range in elevation, and are both attractive, ornamental species.

**DESCRIPTION: Height** of this evergreen shrub to 3 m (10 ft.); **leaves** alternate, compound, glossy, evergreen, leaflets usually 5 (sometimes 3 or 7), with 5 to 10 spines along the margins, leaflets commonly 2 or more times longer than wide, terminal leaflet longer than other leaflets (2.5 to 6 cm, 1 to 2.5 in.), with a long, tapering tip; **flowers** with 6 yellow petals, 6 to 9 sepals and 6 stamens, occurring in loose, few-flowered clusters; **fruit** a juicy, blood-red berry.

**DISTRIBUTION:** Central and southern New Mexico, west to Arizona, east to Texas, north to Colorado, south to Mexico.

**HABITAT:** Dry, sunny slopes and plains, at elevations from 4,500 to 6,800 ft. (1,370 to 2,070 m).

**CREEPING OREGON-GRAPE**
*Berberis repens*
Barberry Family (Berberidaceae)
**Synonym:** *Mahonia repens*
**Related Species: Desert Oregon-Grape,** *Berberis fremontii*
       **Red Oregon-Grape,** *Berberis haematocarpa*

  Creeping Oregon-Grape, because it spreads readily from underground rhizomes, is an excellent ground cover and erosion fighter. Its leaves are evergreen and holly-like, turning red, yellow or purple in the fall. The fragrant, yellow flowers appear very early in the spring. Birds and mammals feed on the fruits, and they can also be made into jellies. Herbalists call this plant *Yerba de Sangre*, and use a tea from the roots to stimulate the liver. It can also be used to treat anemia and aid in protein digestion. Native Americans used the stems for a yellow dye.

**DESCRIPTION: Height** of this small evergreen plant to 0.5 m (20 in.), plants trailing and spreading close to the ground; **leaves** holly-like, leathery, evergreen, alternate, compound, leaflets 3 to 7 per leaf, 3 to 9 cm (1.25 to 3.5 in.) in length, oval to ovate or oblong, leaves blue to dull green on upper surface, smooth and gray-green on lower surface, spines on leaf margins; **flowers** fragrant, with 6 yellow petals and 6 sepals in dense clusters at the ends of branches; **fruit** a berry, bluish to black with a whitish bloom, ovoid to spheroid in shape.

**DISTRIBUTION:** Widespread in New Mexico, west to Arizona and California, east to Texas, north to Colorado and Canada, south to Mexico.

**HABITAT:** Dry, shady pine forests at 6,200 to 10,000 ft. (1,890 to 3,050 m).

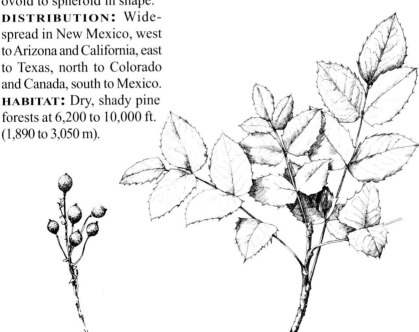

## MOUNTAIN SNOWBERRY, ROUNDLEAF SNOWBERRY
*Symphoricarpos rotundifolius*
Honeysuckle Family (Caprifoliaceae)
**Synonym:** *Symphoricarpos oreophilus*

Mountain Snowberry is a good shrub for attracting wildlife. Deer browse the foliage, and birds and small mammals eat the fruits. Its thicket-forming growth habit also makes it ideal for wildlife cover. The common name Snowberry is derived from its long-lasting, waxy, white fruits for which it is often cultivated. It can be propagated from seeds and from cuttings, but because Mountain Snowberry often spreads by root suckers, it is useful for erosion control on steep banks. The roots have been used medicinally.

**DESCRIPTION: Height** of this deciduous, much-branched shrub to 1 m (3 ft.); **bark** shredding; young twigs smooth and hairless; **leaves** opposite, simple, oval, 1 to 3 cm (0.5 to 1 in.) long, leaf margins entire or toothed, lower leaf surface paler than upper surface and prominently veined; **flowers** tubular, white to pink, 10 to 15 mm (about 0.5 in.) in length, borne separately or in pairs; **fruit** a white, oval, berry-like drupe.

**DISTRIBUTION:** Common over the western and northern parts of New Mexico, west to Arizona and Nevada, north to Colorado, east to Texas, south to Mexico.

**HABITAT:** Pine forests, stream banks, and other moist sites at elevations of 6,000 to 10,000 ft. (1,830 to 3,050 m).

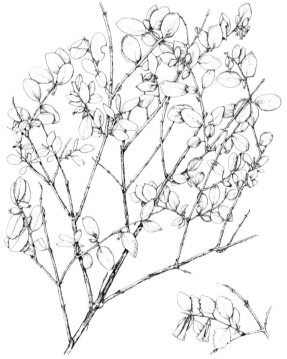

## FOUR-WINGED SALTBUSH
*Atriplex canescens*
Goosefoot Family (Chenopodiaceae)

With Four-winged Saltbush, male and female flowers appear on separate plants. The female plants, with their distinctive four-winged fruits, are easy to identify. Male plants are less conspicuous. Four-winged Saltbush grows in a wide variety of habitats, and is very drought resistant. For these reasons, it is often planted in reclamation projects and for erosion control. Four-winged Saltbush flowers from June to September and the leaves remain on the plant throughout the winter. The salty-tasting foliage provides forage for deer and antelope, and its seeds provide sustenance for birds and rodents. Native Americans used leaves and new shoots for greens, and ground the seeds into meal. Hopis used this species as a leavening agent for baking bread. The leaves provide a yellow dye.

**DESCRIPTION: Height** of this evergreen shrub to 2.5 m (8 ft.) at maturity; **stems** erect, covered with small, grayish, bran-like scales; **leaves** grayish-green, entire, sessile, linear to elliptic to oblong, 1 to 5 cm (0.5 to 2 in.) long, covered with scales; **flowers,** male and female, borne on separate individual plants, male flowers bright yellow to cream-colored, in small clusters, female flowers inconspicuous, borne in small clusters; **fruits** borne on female plants only, seeds encased in four papery, light green, wing-like bracts.

**DISTRIBUTION:** Statewide in New Mexico, north to Colorado and Canada, west to Arizona, Oregon, Utah and California, east to Texas and Oklahoma, south to Mexico.

**HABITAT:** Alkaline soils from the alkali flats, to hilly grasslands and plains, and piñon-juniper woodlands, at elevations of 3,000 to 6,800 ft. (910 to 2,070 m).

## WINTERFAT, WHITE SAGE
*Krascheninnikovia lanata*
Goosefoot Family (Chenopodiaceae)
**Synonyms:** *Ceratoides lanata, Eurotia lanata*

     Winterfat really stands out in the fall, when its fuzzy white to pinkish fruits appear, fluffy and conspicuous, at the tips of the branches. Planted for control of soil erosion, this species also has great potential as an ornamental, and works well in dried flower arrangements. As its common name implies, Winterfat is valuable as winter feed for sheep and cattle. It is also browsed by elk, deer and rabbits, and will attract birds to your garden. The species name, *lanata*, means "wooly," and refers to the overall white-hairiness of the plant. Winterfat grows quickly, and once established, requires no watering. Native Americans applied the powdered root to burns and treated fevers with a decoction of the leaves.

**DESCRIPTION: Height** of this perennial shrub, woody only at the base, to 1 m (3 ft.); **branches** whitish, densely covered with straight and star-shaped hairs; **leaves** alternate, clustered, sessile, linear to oblong with rolled-under margins, 1 to 4 cm (0.5 to 1.5 in.) long, densely hairy; **flowers** borne in clusters in the leaf axils or in clusters at the ends of the branches; **fruits** united into a two-beaked tube, covered with tufts of straight, long, whitish hairs.

**DISTRIBUTION:** Throughout most of New Mexico, north to Colorado and Canada, west to Arizona, Utah and California, east to Texas.

**HABITAT:** Dry hills and plains at elevations of 4,800 to 6,500 ft. (1,460 to 1,980 m).

## RED-OSIER DOGWOOD
*Cornus sericea*
Dogwood Family (Cornaceae)
**Synonyms:** *Cornus stolonifera, Swida stolonifera*

The combination of Dogwood's dark red bark, white flowers and fruits, and reddish leaves in autumn make it a natural for a native plant garden. It can form thickets, providing a privacy screen for your yard. Many species of birds eat the seeds; deer, elk and rabbits browse the foliage. "Osier" refers to the flexible, willow-like twigs, which are used in basketry.

**DESCRIPTION: Height** of this deciduous shrub to 2 m (6.5 ft.); **twigs** dark red to reddish-brown, slender and smooth; **leaves** opposite, entire, 5 to 9 cm (2 to 3.5 in.) long, elliptic, lanceolate to ovate, upper leaf surface dark green, lower surface covered with a whitish bloom; **flowers** white to yellowish, with 4 petals, 4 sepals and 4 stamens, borne in flat-topped, open clusters; **fruit** a white, berry-like drupe.

**DISTRIBUTION:** Western two-thirds of New Mexico, north to Colorado and Canada, west to Arizona, Utah and California, south to Mexico.

**HABITAT:** Near streams and wet areas, from the foothills to the subalpine zone at 5,500 to 9,000 ft. (1,680 to 2,740 m).

## MANZANITA, POINT-LEAF MANZANITA
*Arctostaphylos pungens*
Heath Family (Ericaceae)
**Related Species: Kinnikinnick**, *Arctostaphylos uva-ursi*

Manzanita, with its tiny, pink, bell-like flowers, evergreen leaves, twisted branches and smooth, red bark, is one of the most beautiful shrubs of the Southwest. Its branches sometimes take root where they touch the ground, forming dense thickets that are useful for preventing erosion. The flowers attract hummingbirds, and many mammals (including black bears) and birds feed on Manzanita fruits. In Mexico, the "little apples" are made into a delicious jelly. A tea made from the leaves is used to treat bladder infections and stomach problems, and is applied topically to relieve rheumatism and arthritis. Kinnikinnick, another species in the genus *Arctostaphylos,* was mixed with tobacco and smoked by Native Americans and early settlers. The stems, berries and leaves of Manzanita are sometimes used for Christmas decorations, and dyes of tan, yellow, gold and dark olive can be obtained from the plant.

**DESCRIPTION: Height** of this evergreen shrub 1 to 3 m (3 to 10 ft.), erect and often spreading to 1 m (3 ft.) or more in width; **stems** often twisted, mahogany to reddish-brown and flaky; **leaves** persistent through winter, alternate, simple, leathery, erect, elliptic to lanceolate, sharp pointed at the tip, to 3 cm (1 in.) in length and to 2 cm (0.75 in.) in width; **flowers** white to pink, small, nodding, urn-shaped, less than 1 cm (0.5 in.) in length, inflorescence a crowded raceme; **fruit** a smooth, spherical, reddish to dark brown, several-seeded, berry-like drupe.

**DISTRIBUTION:** Western third of New Mexico, west to Arizona and California, east to Texas, south to Mexico.

**HABITAT:** Well drained, dry, rocky slopes at elevations of 4,500 to 8,000 ft. (1,370 to 2,440 m).

# KINNIKINNICK
*Arctostaphylos uva-ursi*
Heath Family (Ericaceae)
**Related Species: Point-leaf Manzanita,** *Arctostaphylos pungens*

Like its relative Manzanita, Kinnikinnick has delicate, pink, urn-shaped flowers. The bark peels off in conspicuous flakes, revealing red-brown, varnished-looking branches. In addition to being beautiful, this species is a valuable ground cover for rocky slopes, sandy banks, and other areas in need of stabilization. Where the branches touch the ground, they root at the nodes, forming mats that help hold the soil. Kinnikinnick is an Indian word for one of many tobacco substitutes, but is most frequently used for this species. Another common name for this species is Bear-berry, and this is also the translation of its scientific name (*Arkto* = bear, *staphylo* = bunch of grapes, *uva* = grape, and *ursi* = bear). Many species of birds, as well as sheep and deer, use this species for food.

**DESCRIPTION: Height** of this low, creeping, evergreen shrub to about 15 cm (6 in.), with branches rooting at the nodes, and forming dense mats; **bark** on older twigs shredding into long thin strips; **leaves** alternate, simple, thick and leathery, obovate to oblanceolate to oblong-spatulate, margins entire and turned under; **flowers** urn-shaped, white to pink, borne singly or in racemes; **fruit** a round, red berry.

**DISTRIBUTION:** Northern and westcentral New Mexico, high elevations in the western states and Canada.

**HABITAT:** Partially shaded, often semi-dry slopes throughout coniferous forests of the subalpine and montane zones at elevations of 6,500 to 10,000 ft. (1,980 to 3,050 m).

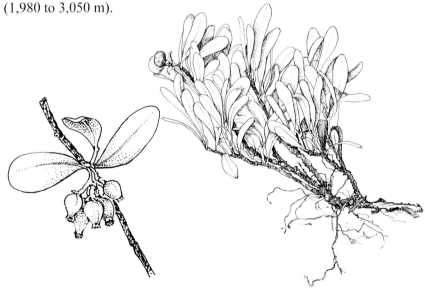

## INDIGO BUSH, FALSE INDIGO
*Amorpha fruticosa*
Legume Family (Fabaceae)

With its dark purple flower spikes and contrasting gold anthers, Indigo Bush is very distinctive and attractive. Given additional water, *Amorpha* should do well in a shady part of your garden, and will flower from May to July. It is useful for erosion control, and is rarely attacked by insects or disease. Birds and other wildlife eat the seeds, and butterflies are attracted to the flowers. There are several varieties of *Amorpha fruticosa*, with differences in leaflet shape and flower color.

**DESCRIPTION: Height** of this deciduous shrub to 2 m (6.5 ft.) at maturity; **leaves** alternate, compound, to 20 cm (8 in.) long, with 9 to 25 leaflets; the leaflets 2 to 4 cm (0.75 to 1.5 in.) long, oval, elliptic or oblong, leaflets dark green on upper surface, paler below; **inflorescence** to 15 cm (6 in.) long, comprised of several spikes in a cluster, one petal per flower, deep purple in color, stamens 10, extending beyond the petals; **fruit** a legume containing two seeds.

**DISTRIBUTION:** Southern New Mexico, north to Colorado and Canada, west to Arizona, Utah and California, east to New England, south to Mexico.

**HABITAT:** Moist soils in canyons and along stream margins, at elevations of 4,500 to 6,000 ft. (1,370 to 1,830 m).

## FAIRY DUSTER, MESQUITILLA
*Calliandra eriophylla*
Legume Family (Fabaceae)

A showy, small shrub of the desert, Fairy Duster bears flowers that look like little powder puffs. They are pink, with long, showy stamens that are white at the base and reddish purple at the tips. *Calliandra* means "beautiful stamens." Even the pods are conspicuous: upon ripening, they split and the halves stand widely apart for a long time. This low shrub is a perfect ground cover, spreading by underground stems, and helping to hold dry soil at low elevations. Fairy Duster has very low water requirements. The leaves may wilt when it's extremely dry, but will revive after a rain. Many animals feed on the foliage and seeds, and hummingbirds visit the flowers, which bloom from March through May.

**DESCRIPTION: Height** of this low creeping shrub to 30 cm (12 in.); **leaves** alternate, even doubly pinnately compound, leaves with 1-4 pairs of pinnae, and leaflets 5-12 pairs on each pinna; **flowers** pink to deep red, ar-

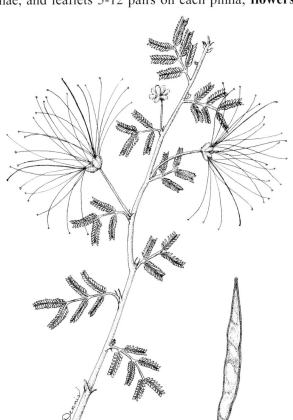

ranged in loose heads with 20 or more stamens extending beyond the flowers; **fruit** a silky-hairy legume, 3 to 8 cm (1.25 to 3.5 in.) long.

**DISTRIBUTION:** Southwest corner of New Mexico, west to Arizona and California, east to Texas, south to Mexico.

**HABITAT:** Dry gravelly slopes and mesas at 4,000 to 5,000 ft. (1,220 to 1.520 m) in elevation.

## FEATHER INDIGOBUSH
*Dalea formosa*
Legume Family (Fabaceae)

"*Formosa*" is Latin for "beautiful," and this plant lives up to its name. Four of its five petals are purple to rose-colored, and the fifth is bright yellow, turning maroon. The lobes of the calyx are feathery, hence the common name. Feather Dalea is conspicuous when it flowers in early spring and after the summer rains. Hispanics use this species to treat rheumatism. Pueblo Indians made a tea of the flowering branches to relieve aches and growing pains. The Hopis used Feather Dalea to treat influenza and virus infections. Deer browse the foliage, and rodents eat the seeds.

**DESCRIPTION: Height** of this deciduous shrub to 70 cm (28 in.); **leaves** alternate, compound, with 5 to 11 leaflets; leaflets 1 to 3 mm (less than 0.25 in.) long, glandular-dotted beneath; **flowers** with one yellow and four purple petals, calyx glandular, with long feathery calyx lobes; **fruit** a hairy, glandular legume.

**DISTRIBUTION:** Widespread throughout New Mexico, north to Colorado, east to Texas and Oklahoma, west to Arizona, south to Mexico.

**HABITAT:** Dry hills, mesas and canyons at 3,500 to 7,000 ft. (1,070 to 2,130 m).

# MESQUITE, HONEY MESQUITE
*Prosopis glandulosa*
Legume Family (Fabaceae)
**Synonym:** *Prosopis juliflora* var. *glandulosa*

The roots of Mesquite sometimes reach a depth of 60 ft., allowing them to flourish where many plants could not survive. Mesquite wood makes excellent, fragrant firewood, and trees cut for wood sprout again. Native Americans of the Southwest made extensive use of mesquite, utilizing every part of the plant. The seed pods, ripening just before the summer rains, were one of the few foods available in early summer. Fresh pods, minus the hard seeds, are sweet and edible right off the plant. Dried pods were ground into flour, and baked into rolls and cakes. The hard, water-resistant wood was used for a variety of objects, including bowls, weapons, cradles and more. The root fibers were twisted into cordage. Medicines and teas were made from the leaves. Pitch from the bark was used to mend and paint pottery, made into candy, and used as a dye. Mesquite honey is highly prized. A tea of the pods and leaves is an excellent eyewash.

**DESCRIPTION: Height** of this thorny deciduous shrub to 3 m (10 ft.); branches crooked, knotty and drooping and the crown rounded, single or paired straight spines, to 0.7 cm (3 in.) long, appearing at nodes on the branches; **leaves** alternate, bipinnately compound (two-branched), total leaf 6 to 18 cm (2.5 to 7 in.) in length, 8 to 14 leaflet pairs per segment of the bipinnately compound leaf; leaflets linear in shape, 1 to 2 cm (less than 1 in.) in length, leaf margins entire; **flowers** perfect, cream-colored or yellowish, borne in dense spikes; **fruits** are legumes borne in loose clusters, legumes 7 to 20 cm (3 to 8 in.) in length and constricted between the seeds.

**DISTRIBUTION:** Widely scattered over the southern two-thirds of New

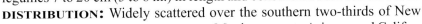

Mexico, west to Arizona and California, east to Texas, Oklahoma and Kansas, south to Mexico.

**HABITAT:** Grasslands, hillsides and along watercourses at 3,000 to 5,500 ft. (910 to 1,680 m) in elevation.

**CONSERVATION CONSIDERATIONS:** The invasion of mesquites into former grasslands of the Southwest is the result of overgrazing a century ago.

142

## BROOM DALEA
*Psorothamnus scoparius*
Legume Family (Fabaceae)
**Synonym:** *Dalea scoparia*

Broom Dalea is a perfect choice for sandy soils in low elevations. Its gray-green foliage, speckled with orange glands, and contrasting dark blue flowers are very striking. This shrub can be used in erosion control, helping to hold sandy soils. Broom Dalea flowers from June to September. *Scoparius* means "broom-like," and refers to the stems. A fascinating walkingstick insect (*Diapheromera* sp.) lives only on this plant. When disturbed, it secretes a lovely blue-purple fluid - the same color as the flowers - from the joints of its legs.

**DESCRIPTION: Height** of this deciduous shrub to 1.5 m (5 ft.); stems grayish; **leaves** alternate, linear to spatulate, 0.5 to 1.9 cm (to 0.75 in.) long, glandular-dotted; **flowers** dark blue, borne in dense spikes or weak heads, at the ends of the branches 2 to 7 cm (0.75 to 3 in.) above the leaves of the plant; **fruit** a hairy, glandular-dotted legume.

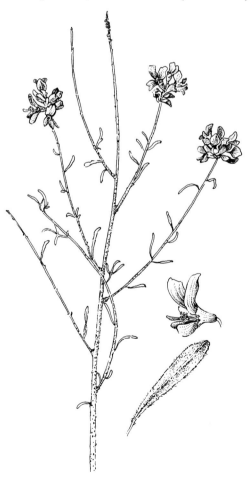

**DISTRIBUTION:** Central and southwestern New Mexico, west to Arizona, east to Texas, south to Mexico.

**HABITAT:** Sandy soils from the hills and dunes of southwestern New Mexico from 5,300 ft. (1,620 m) to the banks of the Rio Grande at 3,500 ft. (1,070 m).

# MESCAL-BEAN SOPHORA, TEXAS MOUNTAIN LAUREL
*Sophora secundiflora*
Legume Family (Fabaceae)

Mescal-Bean Sophora is often planted as an ornamental, and with good reason. It has lustrous leaves, showy, fragrant, purple flowers in long spikes, and large, velvety seed pods. Inside the pods are several large, hard, bright red seeds, which Native Americans used in jewelry. The seeds and flowers are said to contain alkaloids that are poisonous. Because of this property, Native Americans crushed the seeds, and mixed the powder with the beverage mescal to produce intoxication, delirium, and sleep.

**DESCRIPTION: Height** of this evergreen shrub (sometimes a small tree) to 3 m (10 ft.); **leaves** alternate, compound, with 5 to 11 leaflets per leaf; leaflets firm, glossy, to 2 cm (0.75 in.) wide; **flowers** purple, in terminal or axillary racemes; **fruit** a legume, woody and hard, densely brown pubescent, constricted between the seeds, 5 to 12 cm (2 to 5 in.) long, containing 1 to 8 large, bright red seeds.

**DISTRIBUTION:** Southeast New Mexico, east to Texas, south to Mexico.

**HABITAT:** Limestone bluffs and rocky washes at 4,000 to 5,000 ft. (1,220 to 1,520 m).

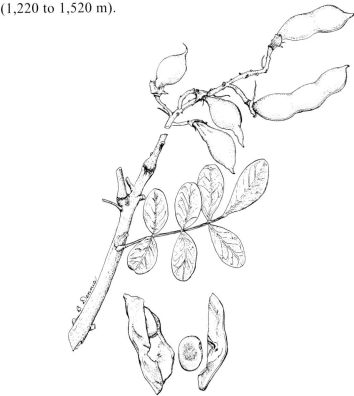

## SILVERLEAF OAK, WHITELEAF OAK
*Quercus hypoleucoides*
Oak Family (Fagaceae)

    This attractive, evergreen species is worthy of cultivation. Silverleaf Oak is easily distinguished from the other oaks by its thick, leathery leaves: the glossy upper surface, the silvery hairiness of the lower surface, and the rolled under leaf margins. The species name, *hypoleucoides*, means "white underneath." Silverleaf Oaks' acorns are consumed by squirrels and birds. Humans too can eat the acorns, but we must first leach out the tannic acid. **DESCRIPTION: Height** of this shrub or tree to 10 m (33 ft.); **bark** black and roughly furrowed; **leaves** persistent through winter, alternate, simple, leathery, lanceolate to elliptic, averaging more than 4.5 cm (1.75 in.) in length at maturity, upper leaf surface dark green or yellow-green and often lustrous, lower leaf surface woolly and white, leaf margin entire and rolled under; **flowers** are catkins, male and female catkins borne on the same tree; **fruits** are acorns.
**DISTRIBUTION:** Southwestern third of New Mexico, west to Arizona, east to Texas, south to Mexico.
**HABITAT:** Oak and coniferous forests, moist canyons and higher slopes at 5,000 to 8,000 ft. (1,520 to 2,440 m) in elevation.

## OCOTILLO
*Fouquieria splendens*
Ocotillo Family (Fouquieriaceae)

Ocotillo is one of the Southwest's most distinctive and conspicuous shrubs. Although its stems are spiny and it grows in the desert, it is not a cactus. During dry spells, the leafless stems look dead. But shortly after rains, the small, bright green leaves appear along the length of the stem, making it look thick and healthy. Ocotillo may leaf out a few times during the warmer months, depending on the timing of rains. The stems of Ocotillo are photosynthetic, enabling the plant to produce enough sugar to survive leafless periods. Its showy, crimson flowers are visited by hummingbirds during their migration from Mexico into the southwestern U.S., and are also pollinated by bees, orioles, finches and other birds. Ocotillo can live up to 200 years. The thorny stems are sometimes set in the ground to build living fences. Many wild populations are being heavily exploited for the commercial landscape trade. Important migration routes for hummingbirds may be distrupted by this practice.

**DESCRIPTION: Height** of this deciduous shrub to 7 m (23 ft.), with many slender, erect, grooved, spiny, cane-like stems arising from the base; **leaves** alternate, simple, oblanceolate to spatulate, thick and leathery, 1.5 to 4 cm (0.5 to 1.5 in.) in length, leaf margins entire; **flowers** bright crimson, showy, to 2.5 cm (1 in.) in length, perfect, tubular, borne in dense clusters at the

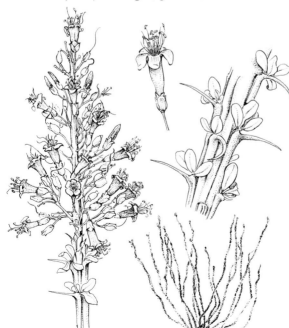

ends of the stems, appearing before the leaves; **fruit** an ovoid capsule producing many winged seeds.

**DISTRIBUTION:** Southern one-third of New Mexico, west to Arizona and California, east to Texas, south to Mexico.

**HABITAT:** Dry, rocky, well-drained soils and south-facing slopes, at elevations of 4,000 to 6,500 ft. (1,220 to 1,980 m).

## GOLDEN CURRANT
*Ribes aureum*
Gooseberry Family (Grossulariaceae)
**Related Species: Wax Currant,** *Ribes cereum*
                              **Orange Gooseberry,** *Ribes pinetorum*
                              **Wolf's Currant,** *Ribes wolfii*

     This species is planted extensively because of its fragrant, bright yellow flowers in early spring, sweet berries, and attractive growth habit. Golden Currant has maple-like leaves that turn red in the fall. Because it prefers partial shade, it is an ideal shrub for planting under a large tree. *Ribes aureum* spreads by underground suckers, and is useful for erosion control. It makes a good privacy screen and provides cover for wildlife. If browsed or pruned, the twigs and foliage become more dense. The flowers, as well as the fruits, can be eaten straight from the bush; most often the fruits are made into jams, pies, and even ice cream. Native Americans mixed dried currants with dried, powdered bison meat to make pemmican. The twigs and leaves of Golden Currant can be used for yellow, brown, gold and olive green dyes.

**DESCRIPTION: Height** of this deciduous shrub to 1.5 m (5 ft.); **branches** gray to brown or reddish, spineless; **leaves** alternate, simple, with three distinct lobes, the lobes coarsely toothed (sometimes entire), leaves orbicular in outline, up to 5 cm (2 in.) wide, upper leaf surface smooth and glossy, lower leaf surface with a few hairs; **flowers** yellow (sometimes tipped with red), borne in racemes, trumpet-shaped, extremely fragrant; **fruit** a smooth, spineless berry, dark red to black at maturity.

**DISTRIBUTION:** Common over much of New Mexico, west to Arizona and California, north to Colorado and Canada, east to Texas.

**HABITAT:**
Stream margins, alluvial areas and moist slopes at 6,500 to 9,000 ft. (1,980 to 2,740 m) in elevation.

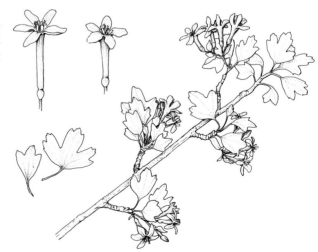

**WAX CURRANT**
*Ribes cereum*
Gooseberry Family (Grossulariaceae)
**Synonym:** *Ribes inebrians*
**Related Species:  Golden Currant,** *Ribes aureum*
**Orange Gooseberry,** *Ribes pinetorum*
**Wolf's Currant,** *Ribes wolfii*

Wax Currant, grown from seeds or cuttings, makes a good ornamental. The foliage is browsed by elk and deer, and the fruits are eaten by bears, rodents, birds and other wildlife. Native Americans ate the berries fresh or dried, mixed with bison meat in pemmican, and also used them to make an intoxicating beverage (the synonym for this species is *Ribes inebrians,* or "inebriating currant"). The flowers of Wax Currant are also edible. Hopis used the berries to relieve stomach aches. The twigs and leaves of Wax Currant can be used for yellow, brown, gold and olive green dyes.
**DESCRIPTION: Height** of this deciduous shrub to 1 m (3 ft.); **branches** crooked, smooth, red-brown, spineless; **leaves** alternate, simple, fragrant, sticky, palmately veined, shallowly 3- to 5-lobed, the lobes toothed, leaves 1 to 3.5 cm (0.5 to 1.5 in.) wide, leaf length and width about the same, leaves orbicular in outline; **flowers** cream-colored or pink, perfect, borne in racemes; **fruit** a red or orange-red berry, borne singly or in small clusters.

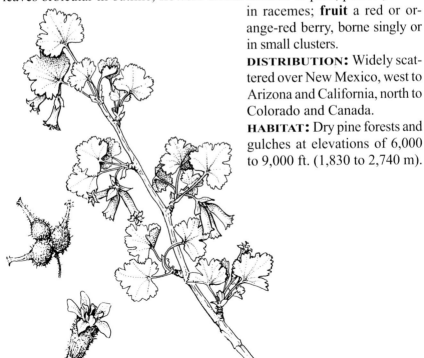

**DISTRIBUTION:** Widely scattered over New Mexico, west to Arizona and California, north to Colorado and Canada.
**HABITAT:** Dry pine forests and gulches at elevations of 6,000 to 9,000 ft. (1,830 to 2,740 m).

## ORANGE GOOSEBERRY
*Ribes pinetorum*
Gooseberry Family (Grossulariaceae)
**Related Species: Golden Currant,** *Ribes aureum*
**Wax Currant**, *Ribes cereum*
**Wolf's Currant**, *Ribes wolfii*

Orange Gooseberry, like its relatives the Currants, is a good shrub for attracting wildlife. Elk and deer browse the foliage, and many mammals and birds eat the fruits. *Arizona Flora* states that *Ribes pinetorum* is "the handsomest wild gooseberry of the state." The specific name, *pinetorum*, refers to its growth in pine forests. Orange Gooseberry blooms from April to September, allowing plenty of time to enjoy its beautiful red-orange flowers. This species can be readily distinguished from the Golden, Wax and Wolf's Currants by its spiny fruits.

**DESCRIPTION: Height** of deciduous shrub to 2 m (6.5 ft.); **stems** bearing 1 to 3 spines at the nodes, older branches reddish brown to gray; **leaves** alternate (but often appearing clustered at the nodes), simple, dark green, 5-lobed, the lobes toothed, 25 to 40 mm wide; **flowers** reddish-orange, up to 18 mm in length; **fruit** a round berry, orange to purplish-red at maturity, covered with bristles.

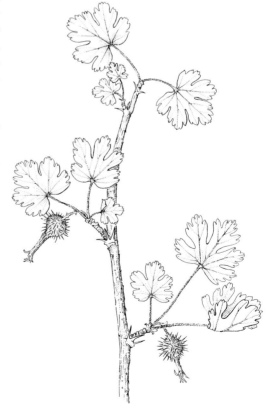

**DISTRIBUTION:** Southwest quarter of New Mexico, west to Arizona.

**HABITAT:** Coniferous forests at elevations of 6,800 to 11,500 ft. (2,070 to 3,500 m).

# WOLF'S CURRANT
*Ribes wolfii*
Gooseberry Family (Grossulariaceae)
**Related Species: Golden Currant,** *Ribes aureum*
**Wax Currant,** *Ribes cereum*
**Orange Gooseberry,** *Ribes pinetorum*

Wolf's Currant has delicate, white, bell-shaped flowers which bloom from May to June. The large, smooth leaves are distinctive and attractive. Birds and small mammals eat the fruits, which can be made into pies and jellies. In its natural habitat, Wolf's Currant is found in damp, shady woods at high elevations. The genus name, *Ribes*, is from an old Danish word, *ribs*, meaning "red currant." *Ribes* is the only genus in the family Grossulariaceae.

**DESCRIPTION: Height** of deciduous shrub to 1.5 m (5 ft.), not spiny; **leaves** alternate (but appearing to be fascicled at the tips of the branches), simple, distinctly 5-lobed, the lobes rounded and toothed, **leaves** 4 to 8 cm wide; **flowers** small, white, in 4 to 8-flowered clusters at the ends of the branches; **fruit** a berry, round and black.

**DISTRIBUTION:** Western two-thirds of New Mexico, north to Colorado, west to Arizona, Utah, Idaho and Washington.

**HABITAT:** Moist woods, often among aspens and conifers, at 7,000 to 11,500 ft. (2,130 to 3,500 m).

150

## CLIFF FENDLERBUSH
*Fendlera rupicola*
Hydrangea Family (Hydrangeaceae)

It's always a delight to come across Cliff Fendlerbush on an inhospitable, rocky hillside. Its flowers, with four spoon-shaped white petals in the form of a cross, are large, numerous, fragrant and showy. The buds are rose-colored, and appear from March to June. Cliff Fendlerbush is resistant to drought, and would do well in a rock garden. The genus is named for Augustus Fendler, a German botanist who collected many plants in the Southwest. In fact, *Rupicola* means "lover of rocks," referring to the plant's rocky habitat. Wildlife browse the foliage.

**DESCRIPTION: Height** of this deciduous, widely branched shrub to 2 m (6.5 ft.); **bark** gray and shredding; **leaves** opposite, sometimes appearing clustered, simple, lanceolate to elliptic, 2 to 4 cm (0.75 to 1.5 in.) long, margins rolled under slightly; **flowers** white, 4 sepals, 4 clawed petals, 8 stamens; **fruit** a conical, pointed capsule, separating into 4 or 5 sections.

**DISTRIBUTION:** South and west New Mexico, east to Texas, north to Colorado, west to Arizona and Utah, south to Mexico.

**HABITAT:** Rocky slopes in the mountains at 5,500 to 8,200 ft. (1,680 to 2,500 m).

# WAXFLOWER
*Jamesia americana*
Hydrangea Family (Hydrangeaceae)

Waxflower has many appealing attributes: reddish, peeling bark, fragrant creamy white flowers in clusters at the branch tips, dark green, velvety, deeply veined leaves, and fruits that persist through winter. In autumn, the leaves turn rose to dark red. *Jamesia* is named for Dr. Edwin James, the physician-botanist who accompanied Major Long on his explorations of the Rocky Mountains in 1820. But this plant was around long before then: fossils of this species from 35 million years ago have been found in southern Colorado.

**DESCRIPTION: Height** of this deciduous shrub to 2 m (6.5 ft.); **bark** reddish brown and peeling; **leaves** opposite, toothed, ovate to oval, 1.5 to 6 cm (to 2.5 in.) long, green on upper surface and whitish-hairy on lower surface; **flowers** with 5 sepals, 5 white petals and 10 stamens; **fruit** a capsule with numerous seeds.

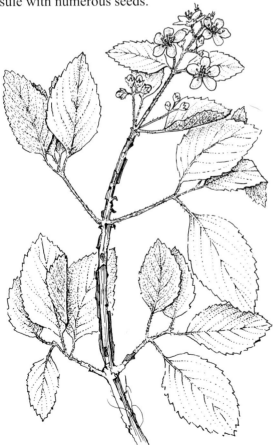

**DISTRIBUTION:** Western two-thirds of New Mexico, north to Colorado, west to Arizona, Utah, Nevada, Wyoming and California. **HABITAT:** Canyons of the mountains at elevations of 6,500 to 10,000 ft. (1,980 to 3,050 m).

152

## BLUE SAGE, SHRUBBY SALVIA
*Salvia pinguifolia*
Mint Family (Lamiaceae)

Blue Sage, because of its hairy leaves and stems, has a pleasant silvery appearance. The scalloped leaves are very fragrant, and have a slightly greasy feeling when rubbed between the fingers. Its bluish purple flowers are borne in whorls around the stem. This shrub has traditionally been used to wean infants from breastfeeding; when the plant was in flower, a tea was made and taken internally. The breasts were also washed with the tea. Volatile oils from *Salvias* are sometimes used to scent creams, soaps and shampoos. Another species in this genus, *Salvia officinalis,* is the sage used for seasoning.

**DESCRIPTION: Height** of this deciduous shrub to 1 m (3 ft.) or more; **stems** and **branches** square in cross section, young stems covered with whitish hairs, older branches becoming smooth, reddish brown to light brown or gray, irregularly shreddy; **leaves** opposite, simple, 2 to 5.5 cm (0.75 to 2 in.) in length, with a leaf stalk up to 2 cm (0.75 in.) long, deltoid to ovate in shape, leaf margins coarsely toothed, upper leaf surface green, lower leaf surface white with hairs; **flowers** blue, irregular, borne in spikes at the ends of the stems; **fruits** are four nutlets occurring together.

**DISTRIBUTION:** Southern and southeastern New Mexico, west to Arizona, east to western Texas, south to Mexico.
**HABITAT:** Dry mesas and hillsides at 3,500 to 7,000 ft. (1,070 to 2,130 m) in elevation.

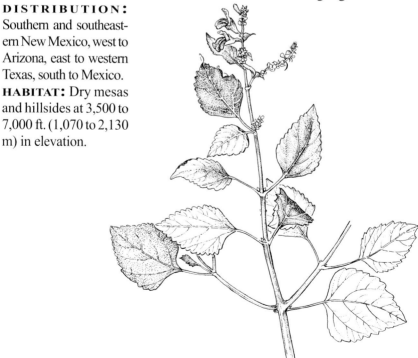

# NEW MEXICO OLIVE, NEW MEXICO FORESTIERA
*Forestiera pubescens*
Olive Family (Oleaceae)
**Synonym:** *Forestiera neomexicana*

New Mexico Olive is an attractive shrub with bright green, glossy leaves which turn yellow in fall. It is tolerant of heat and has low water requirements, although occasional deep watering helps it to grow faster. Since it tends to grow in clumps, New Mexico Olive is useful for screening. If pruned, it can grow into a small tree with an open appearance; when its lower branches are removed, the handsome whitish bark is visible. Although its olive-like fruits taste very bitter to people, they are eaten by songbirds. New Mexico Olive has very hard wood, and is one of many southwestern plants known as ironwood.

**DESCRIPTION: Height** of this deciduous shrub 1 to 3 m (3 to 10 ft.), sometimes a small tree; **branches** sometimes spiny; **leaves** opposite, simple, 1 to 4 cm (0.5 to 1.5 in.) long, spatulate, oblong, obovate or oblanceolate, leaf margins entire or serrate, leaves glossy or with hairs on both surfaces; **flowers** small, inconspicuous, appearing before the leaves, borne in axillary, few-flowered clusters, or solitary at the nodes, unisexual or bisexual, sometimes the male and female flowers borne on separate plants; **fruit** is a purple to black, ellipsoid drupe.

**DISTRIBUTION:** Widely scattered over New Mexico, west to Arizona and California, north to Colorado, east to Texas, south to Mexico.

**HABITAT:** Dry, rocky slopes and desert canyons at 4,000 to 7,000 ft. (1,220 to 2,130 m) in elevation.

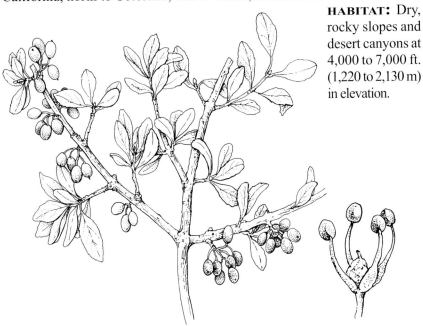

## BUCKBRUSH, FENDLER CEANOTHUS
*Ceanothus fendleri*
Buckthorn Family (Rhamnaceae)
**Related Species: Desert Ceanothus,** *Ceanothus greggii*

Buckbrush's clusters of small, fragrant, white or pinkish flowers are so prolific they almost cover the plant, and it blooms from June to August. It often comes in after a fire, and can form thickets. In cultivation, it is sometimes used in rock gardens & sandbank plantings. *Ceanothus* is well regarded as a honey plant, and is browsed by deer, porcupines and jack rabbits. It contains saponin, which gives the flowers and fruits a soap-like quality. Native Americans made tea from the leaves, and used the fruits for food and medicine.

**DESCRIPTION: Height** of this deciduous shrub to 1 m (3 ft.); **stems** often spine-tipped, young twigs densely hairy, becoming smooth in maturity; **leaves** alternate, simple, elliptic in outline, lower surface white-hairy and with 3 main veins, upper surface green to gray-green and hairy; **flowers** small, white, in clusters at the ends of the branches, 5 petals, 5 sepals, 5 stamens extending beyond petals; **fruit** a 3-lobed, small, dry capsule.

**DISTRIBUTION:** Widely scattered throughout New Mexico, east to Texas, north to Colorado, west to Arizona, Utah and Wyoming, south to Mexico.

**HABITAT:** Dry montane forests, valleys and hillsides, usually in gravelly soil, at 5,500 to 9,500 ft. (1,680 to 2,900 m).

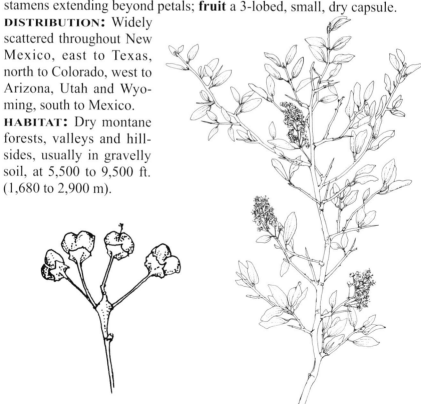

# DESERT CEANOTHUS, DESERT BUCKTHORN
*Ceanothus greggii*
Buckthorn Family (Rhamnaceae)
**Related Species: Buckbrush** or **Fendler Ceanothus,** *Ceanothus fendleri*

In the spring, this species bears such sweet smelling clusters of white flowers that it earns one of its common names, Desert Lilac. *Ceanothus* is extremely drought tolerant and, once established, won't tolerate over-watering. In the wild, deer browse this plant heavily, and it is unusual to see a specimen that they haven't touched. Rodents and quail eat the small seeds. Desert Ceanothus, called "red root" by herbalists, is used as a treatment for syphilis and is said to have purgative properties. The leaves and flowers, boiled for five minutes, make an excellent tea. Desert Ceanothus flowers have been used in Mexico to make a cleansing lather for washing clothes. A red dye is obtained from the roots. Another species in this genus, *Ceanothus americanus,* was used as a tea substitute during the American Revolution.

**DESCRIPTION: Height** of this deciduous (evergreen in some locations) shrub to 2 m (6.5 ft.); **branches** rigid, spineless, felt-covered, pinkish when young, becoming gray with age; **leaves** opposite, simple, leathery, upper leaf surface shiny green, lower leaf surface grayish green, less than 1.5 cm (0.5 in.) in length, elliptic or oblanceolate in shape, leaf margins entire to only slightly toothed; **flowers** white (sometimes bluish or pinkish), sweet-scented, with 5 spoon-shaped, hooded petals, in dense terminal or axillary clusters; **fruit** is a 3-lobed capsule (some authorities call it a drupe).

**DISTRIBUTION:** Southern portion of New Mexico, west to Arizona and California, east to Texas, south to Mexico.

**HABITAT:** Dry mountains and canyons at 4,500 to 7,000 ft. (1,370 to 2,130 m) in elevation.

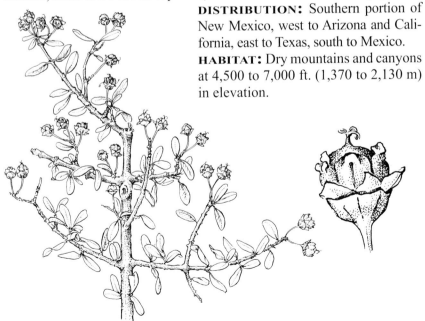

**156**

## BIRCH-LEAF BUCKTHORN, COFFEEBERRY
*Frangula betulifolia*
Buckthorn Family (Rhamnaceae)
**Synonym:** *Rhamnus betulifolia*

Although the common name seems to indicate otherwise, this shrub has no thorns. Its leaves are birch-like and attractive, with prominent veins. Birchleaf Buckthorn is a fairly common sight along the streams of the Southwest. The fruits are bitter, but are eaten by many species of wildlife, and the young foliage is browsed by mule deer. Birch-leaf Buckthorn, called *Cascara Sagrada* by Spanish-speaking herbalists, contains cascarin, a mild laxative. It is also useful for relief of nausea and upset stomach. The berries can be made into an unsatisfactory substitute for coffee.

**DESCRIPTION: Height** of this deciduous shrub to 3 m (10 ft.), sometimes a tree up to 5 m (17 ft.); **leaves** alternate, simple, thin, 5 to 15 cm (2 to 6 in.) in length and 2.5 to 4 cm (1 to 1.5 in.) in width, elliptic to ovate or oblong, leaf margins serrate (rarely entire), green to dark green on both leaf surfaces, upper surface smooth and lustrous, lower leaf surface very finely haired and conspicuously veined; **flowers** small, greenish, in axillary clusters, appearing after the leaves; **fruit** a black to dark purple drupe, almost round, commonly 3-seeded.

**DISTRIBUTION:** Southwestern New Mexico, west to Arizona, Utah and Nevada, east to Texas, south to Mexico.

**HABITAT:** Moist canyons and along streams at 4,500 to 7,500 ft. (1,370 to 2,300 m) in elevation.

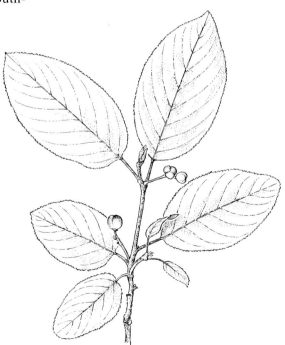

## SHADBUSH, CLUSTER SERVICEBERRY
*Amelanchier pumila*
Rose Family (Rosaceae)
**Synonyms:** *Amelanchier alnifolia* var. *pumila*
         *Amelanchier polycarpa*
**Related Species: Utah Serviceberry,** *Amelanchier utahensis*

    Shadbush has fragrant white flowers in early spring, blueberry-like berries in summer, and yellow or red foliage in the fall. It has low water requirements and is long lived. Shadbush is also a good shrub for attracting wildlife: small mammals and birds eat the fruits, and the foliage is browsed by sheep, goats and deer. The fruits of Cluster Serviceberry are often used for jams and pies, although their numerous seeds make them less than ideal to work with. Native Americans ground the dried berries and mixed them with venison or buffalo meat to make pemmican. The slender, straight branches, after peeling, are ideal for the weaving of large carrying baskets.

    Because of hybridization, there is some confusion among the different species in the genus *Amelanchier*, but it is possible to distinguish between Shadbush and Utah Serviceberry. The latter has hairs on its buds, leaves and twigs, and the former lacks hairs. *Amelanchier pumila* has a more extensive range than *A. utahensis.*

**DESCRIPTION: Height** of this deciduous shrub 1 to 3 m (3 to 10 ft.); **leaves** alternate, simple, smooth, oval to orbicular, thick, deeper green above, paler green on lower leaf surface, leaf margins toothed on upper two thirds of blade, 2 to 5 cm (0.75 to 2 in.) in length and 1.5 to 4.2 cm (0.5 to 1.5 in.)

in width; **flowers** white, 5-petaled, borne in racemes at the ends of the stems; **fruit** a pome, purple, 5 to 15 mm (to 0.5 in.) in length, with a waxy coating that is easily wiped off.

**DISTRIBUTION:** Northern two-thirds of New Mexico, west to Arizona and California, north to Colorado, Oregon and Montana.

**HABITAT:** Wet meadows, along stream margins and on forested mountain slopes at elevations of 7,000 to 9,000 ft. (2,130 to 2,740 m).

## MOUNTAIN MAHOGANY
*Cercocarpus montanus*
Rose Family (Rosaceae)

Mountain Mahogany is browsed heavily by bighorn sheep and deer. Protected from wildlife, however, it can grow into a small tree, perfect for yards where space is at a premium. In the fall, Mountain Mahogany is very conspicuous and beautiful because of the fuzzy, spirally twisted tails on the fruits. These tails twist like corkscrews, and drill themselves into the ground, where the seeds can germinate. Mountain Mahogany is drought tolerant and can grow in shade or full sun. The scraped bark adds flavor to Mormon Tea (*Ephedra*). Navajos use the shrub's bark and roots to make a red dye for wool, and the wood is used as a staff to hold the wool. The twigs and leaves yield dyes of tan, brown and gold. Early settlers reportedly used the leafy twigs of Mountain Mahogany to keep bedbugs away. Because the wood is very hard and doesn't splinter, its Spanish name is *palo duro*: hard wood.

**DESCRIPTION: Height** of this shrub to 2 m (6.5 ft.), or sometimes a small tree to 4 m (13 ft.); **bark** gray to brown, fissured when mature; **leaves** alternate, simple, thin, 2.2 to 4 cm (0.75 to 1.5 in.) in length and 1.5 to 3 cm (0.5 to 1 in.) in width, gray or gray-green on upper leaf surface, paler and densely hairy on lower leaf surface, obovate to elliptic, leaf margins toothed on upper half; **flowers** greenish, inconspicuous, bisexual, solitary or in clusters of 2 or 3; **fruit** an achene with a silvery, fuzzy, spirally twisted tail to 7 cm (3 in.) long.

**DISTRIBUTION:** Northern half and southern mountains of New Mexico, west to Arizona, Utah and Wyoming, north to Colorado, east to Texas and Nebraska, south to Mexico.

**HABITAT:** Sunny slopes and dry hillsides in piñon-juniper and mixed coniferous forests, and in aspen communities at 5,500 to 8,500 ft. (1,680 to 2,600 m) in elevation.

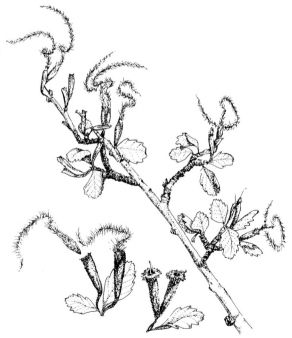

## APACHE PLUME
*Fallugia paradoxa*
Rose Family (Rosaceae)
**Similar Species: Cliffrose,** *Purshia stansburiana*

Apache Plume is a popular ornamental, with attractive rose-like white flowers and pink, feathery fruits occurring on the plant at the same time. It grows well in full sun and is very drought tolerant. Acting as a soil binder, this species is useful for erosion control. The common name "Apache Plume" derives from the fact that the feathery fruits look like feather war bonnets; although war bonnets were created by Plains Indians, the plant grows in Apache country. Apache Plume is good cover for quail and other birds. Bees and butterflies visit the flowers, and it is browsed by deer. Native Americans used the stems of Apache Plume for arrowshafts. The roots and leaves are used as a hair growth stimulant, and the bark and flowers are used like aspirin.

**DESCRIPTION: Height** of this deciduous or evergreen shrub to 2 m (6.5 ft.); **branches** whitish, shredding with age; **leaves** alternate, clustered, simple, with 3 to 7 lobes, 0.6 to 1.4 cm (0.25 to 0.5 in.) in length, **leaves** hairy white on the lower surface, leaf margins rolled under slightly;

**flowers** showy, with 5 white petals, more than 2 cm (0.75 in.) in diameter, pistils 20 or more per flower, stamens numerous; **fruit** an achene with more than 20 feathery, long-lasting, white to pinkish tails.

**DISTRIBUTION:** Southwestern quarter of New Mexico, west to Arizona, north to Colorado, east to Texas, south to Mexico.

**HABITAT:** Dry rocky slopes and arroyos at 4,500 to 7,500 ft. (1,370 to 2,290 m) in elevation.

## ROCK SPIRAEA, OCEAN SPRAY
*Holodiscus dumosus*
Rose Family (Rosaceae)
**Synonym:** *Holodiscus discolor* var. *dumosus*

This is a beautiful, graceful shrub, with fragrant, feathery sprays of flowers at the ends of the branches. The dry, feathery blooms and the seeds remain on the plants into winter. The bark of Rock Spiraea peels off in thin layers, further adding to this plant's charm. The bruised leaves give off a pleasant "green apple" odor, helping to identify the plant. Native Americans formerly used the straight branches for arrows. The one-seeded fruits may be eaten raw or cooked.

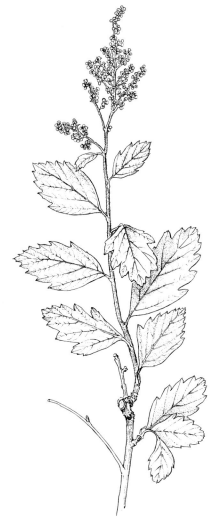

**DESCRIPTION: Height** of this deciduous shrub to 2.5 m (8 ft.); **bark** dark red, becoming gray and shreddy with age; **leaves** alternate, simple, pinnately veined, distinctly toothed, sometimes appearing slightly lobed, obovate to cuneate in outline, 1.5 to 5 cm (0.5 to 2 in.) in length and 1 to 3.5 cm (0.5 to 1.5 in.) in width, upper leaf surface bright green and smooth, lower leaf surface gray and hairy; **flowers** small, white, cream or pink, arranged in a loose and feathery cluster at the ends of the branches; **fruit** an achene, somewhat flattened and hairy.

**DISTRIBUTION:** Widely scattered over the mountainous regions of New Mexico, west to Arizona, California and Oregon, north to Colorado, east to Texas, south to Mexico.

**HABITAT:** Rock outcrops, high plateaus, at the bases of cliffs, and on lava flows at 6,500 to 10,000 ft. (1,980 to 3,050 m) in elevation.

# SHRUBBY CINQUEFOIL
*Pentaphylloides floribunda*
Rose Family (Rosaceae)
**Synonyms:** *Potentilla fruticosa*
*Potentilla floribunda*

Shrubby Cinquefoil is an excellent species for erosion control, and its yellow, rose-like flowers and long blooming season make it a popular ornamental. It can tolerate full sun, drought, poor soil and cold temperatures. Ungulates browse this plant heavily, so it sometimes looks stunted in its natural habitat. Protected in your yard, however, this is a beautiful shrub. A concoction made from Cinquefoil's leaves was used as an arrow poison by the Cheyenne and administered only by holy people. Leaves, stems and flowers yield dyes of light yellow to olive green to almost black. Related species have been used as chewing sticks to clean gums and teeth and as decoctions to relieve toothache.

**DESCRIPTION: Height** of this deciduous shrub to 1 m (3 ft.); **bark** red-brown and shredding; **leaves** alternate, pinnately compound (although at first glance they look palmately compound), 3 to 7 (usually 5) leaflets per leaf, obovate to lanceolate, lower leaf surface silky white, leaf margins entire and somewhat rolled under; **flowers** showy with 5 yellow petals and 20 to 25 stamens; **fruit** an achene, fruit stalk persisting into winter.

**DISTRIBUTION:** Western and northern third of New Mexico, west to Arizona and California, north to Colorado and Canada, east to the Plains states.

**HABITAT:** Dry rocky areas and moist canyons and ravines at 6,500 ft. (1,980 m) to subalpine elevations.

## MOUNTAIN NINEBARK
*Physocarpus monogynus*
Rose Family (Rosaceae)

The common name "ninebark" apparently arises from the fact that the bark continuously shreds off, as if the plant has "nine lives." This shrub is a good choice for an ornamental because of its attractive bark, clusters of tiny white to pinkish flowers, and reddish orange leaves in the fall. Ninebark is also practical because of its tolerance for poor soil, sun or shade, and minimal water. It can be propagated from seed or from cuttings. From the boiled roots, Native Americans made a poultice for treating sores and lesions.

**DESCRIPTION: Height** of this deciduous shrub to 1 m (3 ft.) or more; **bark** peels into papery strips, the outer bark striped dark and light gray-brown, the inner bark pale brown and smooth; **leaves** alternate, simple, palmately 3- or 5-lobed, palmately veined, ovate to round in outline, leaf margins irregularly toothed, upper leaf surface dull dark green, lower surface paler; **flowers** small, with 5 white or pinkish petals and 30 to 40 stamens, 15 to 25 flowers clustered at the ends of the branches; **fruit** an inflated capsule.

**DISTRIBUTION:** Western and northern New Mexico, west to Arizona, north to Colorado, east to Texas and the Plains states.

**HABITAT:** Rocky slopes in dry and open woods at elevations of 6,000 to 10,000 ft. (1,830 to 3,050 m).

## CLIFFROSE
*Purshia stansburiana*
Rose Family (Rosaceae)
**Synonyms:** *Cowania mexicana* var. *stansburiana*
                *Cowania stansburiana*
**Related Species: Apache Plume,** *Fallugia paradoxa*

Cliffrose, a beautiful shrub with evergreen leaves, shredding bark, fragrant rose-like flowers and feathery fruits, is a desirable ornamental. It is also planted for erosion control. Despite its bitterness, the foliage of this plant is heavily browsed by wildlife in the winter months. There is a species of butterfly whose caterpillars eat the leaves of Cliffrose exclusively. The flowers are visited by many species of bees and other insects. A refreshing tea can be made by steeping a handful of leaves in hot water for a few minutes. Native Americans used strips of the inner bark to weave clothing, sandals, rope and mats, and made arrow shafts from the stems. Cliffrose and Apache Plume, both members of the Rose Family, are quite similar in appearance. Cliffrose's flowers are smaller than Apache Plume's (less than 1.5 cm in diameter versus more than 2.0 cm), and are yellow to cream-colored, while Apache Plume's flowers are white.

**DESCRIPTION: Height** of this evergreen shrub to 2 m (6.5 ft.); young **twigs** reddish-brown, older twigs gray and shredding; **leaves** alternate,

simple, thick, leathery and resinous, pinnately lobed with 3 to 9 lobes, 0.6 to 1.4 cm (to 0.5 in.) in length, leaf margins rolled under, leaf surfaces dotted with glands; **flowers** yellow or cream-colored, fragrant, borne singly at the ends of branches; **fruit** an achene with 5 to 10 feathery tails up to 5 cm (2 in.) long.

**DISTRIBUTION:** Western third of New Mexico, west to Arizona and California, north to Colorado, south to Mexico.

**HABITAT:** Dry rocky hillsides and plateaus in high deserts, grasslands and oak-piñon-juniper communities at 3,000 to 8,000 ft. (910 to 2,440 m) in elevation.

164

## WOOD'S ROSE
*Rosa woodsii*
Rose Family (Rosaceae)
**Synonyms:** *Rosa arizonica*
        *Rosa fendleri*

    *Rosa woodsii* is the most common of the several species of wild roses in the genus *Rosa*, which are difficult to tell apart. Compounding the problem is the fact that these roses often hybridize with one another. But no matter which species of native rose you plant, they all share the same qualities: fragrant, showy flowers, bristly stems and red fruits. A good source of vitamin C, rose hips can be eaten raw, stewed or candied, and can also be made into tea, jam and wine. They are often used in vitamins, tablets and syrups, although the amount of synthetic ascorbic acid is generally much greater than the rose hip content. Rose petals are pleasant tasting and can be used in salads. The volatile oil of rose is used for scenting creams, salves, soaps, shampoos, and, of course, perfumes. Medicinally, the leaves and flowers are used as an eyewash. A tea made from the flowers is taken to reduce high fevers, and is also rubbed on the limbs for this purpose. Rose hips, twigs, leaves and blossoms yield dyes of yellow to brown to green. Many species of birds and mammals eat the fruits, and wildlife use the plant for cover.

**DESCRIPTION: Height** of this deciduous shrub to 1.5 m (5 ft.); **stems** with numerous bristles, reddish-brown becoming gray with age; **leaves** alternate, pinnately compound, leaflets 5 to 9, commonly 7, leaflets thin, elliptic to obovate in shape, leaf margins serrate to entire near the base; **flowers** showy and pink with numerous stamens, about 3 cm (1 in.) in diameter, 3 or more flowers in a cluster; **fruit** a red, berry-like hip.

**DISTRIBUTION:** Western two-thirds of New Mexico, west to Arizona, north to Colorado and Canada, east to Texas.

**HABITAT:** Sandy soils, rocky ravines, stream banks, open prairies or near the margins of woods at 4,500 to 9,500 ft. (1,370 to 2,900 m) in elevation.

## THIMBLE RASPBERRY, THIMBLEBERRY
*Rubus parviflorus*
Rose Family (Rosaceae)
**Synonym:** *Rubacer parviflorus*

This shrub lacks spines and has showy, rose-like, fragrant flowers. Although the species name *parviflorus* means "small flowered," Thimble Raspberry's flowers are among the largest in this genus. Many species of birds and mammals eat the berries, and humans make them into jellies. Raspberry leaves have astringent properties and so are used to treat mouth sores and inflammation of mucous membranes of the throat. A tea made from raspberry leaves can be applied to wounds, and moistened leaves used as a poultice. Cold raspberry tea is said to give immediate relief to persons suffering from diarrhea and various stomach ailments. The bark from another species in this genus, *Rubus spectabilis,* is placed in the teeth to relieve toothache. As with many leafy greens, raspberry leaves contain vitamin C. The genus *Rubus* contains the following edible fruits: raspberry, thimbleberry, salmonberry, loganberry, boysenberry, blackberry, and others.

**DESCRIPTION: Height** of this deciduous, spineless shrub 1 to 2 m (3 to 6.5 ft.); outer **bark** gray-brown, shredding to reveal inner layer of red-brown bark; twigs rigid, pale brown, mottled and streaked with dark brown; **leaves** alternate, simple, large, averaging 8 to 30 cm (3.5 to 12 in.) wide, 5-lobed, palmately veined, leaf margins serrate, dark green above, paler below; **flowers** showy, with five white, rounded petals, 2 to 9 flowers in a cluster; **fruit** a red raspberry-like drupelet.

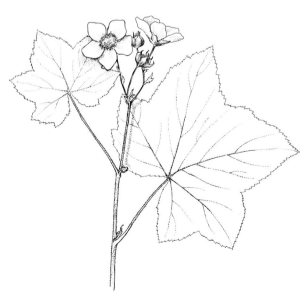

**DISTRIBUTION:** Western two thirds of New Mexico, west to Arizona and California, north to Colorado and Canada.

**HABITAT:** Margins of woods, along stream banks and in moist shaded canyons at 7,000 to 10,000 ft. (2,130 to 3,050 m) in elevation.

**166**

## COYOTE WILLOW, SANDBAR WILLOW
*Salix exigua*
Willow Family (Salicaceae)
**Synonym:** *Salix interior*
**Related Species: Bluestem Willow**, *Salix irrorata*

    Coyote Willow is one of New Mexico's most widespread and common willows. Willows tolerate most types of soil, but must have water. They leaf out early in the spring and retain their leaves until late fall. Reproduction by creeping rootstocks allows this shrub to form thickets that help prevent erosion. *Salix exigua* is a short-lived species, lasting only 20 to 50 years. As with the other willows, Coyote Willow provides cover for wildlife, browse for deer and elk, and food and dam material for beaver. Native Americans have been using willows medicinally for over 2,000 years. The leaves and roots of willows and cottonwoods contain salicylic acid, the active ingredient of aspirin. Willow twigs are popular for making baskets. Other species in the genus *Salix* have been used for wicker furniture. Willow twigs and leaves yield dyes varying from light yellow to greenish gold.

**DESCRIPTION: Height** of this deciduous, several-stemmed shrub from 0.5 to 3 m (20 to 120 in.), sometimes a small tree to 6 m (20 ft.); **branches** reddish, becoming ashy gray with age; **leaves** alternate, simple, linear to lanceolate, 3 to 14 cm (1 to 5.5 in.) in length and 2 to 12 mm (to 0.5 in.) in width, leaf margins entire or with widely spaced teeth, upper leaf surface dull green, lower leaf surface silvery; **flowers** appearing after the leaves, male and female flowers borne on separate plants, male flowers in densely flowered catkins 0.9 to 6 cm (0.5 to 2.5 in.) in length, female flowers in loosely flowered catkins, 2 to 8 cm (0.75 to 3.5 in.) in length; **fruit** a capsule, 4 to 5 mm (less than 0.25 in.) in length.

**DISTRIBUTION:** Widespread over most of New Mexico, west to Arizona and California, north to Colorado and Canada, east to Texas and the Plains states, south to Mexico.

**HABITAT:** Stream banks, river sandbars and roadside ditches, at 3,500 to 7,500 ft. (1,070 to 2,300 m) in elevation.

# BLUESTEM WILLOW
*Salix irrorata*
Willow Family (Salicaceae)
**Related Species: Sandbar Willow,** *Salix exigua*

Willows are beautiful and graceful shrubs, enhancing any area that has sufficient water. Like Coyote Willow, Bluestem Willow is used by wildlife for food and cover, and by beaver for dam material. Bluestem Willow, found in lower elevations, and Blue Willow, at high altitudes, are so similar that they may in fact be only one species. Willows leaf out early in the spring and retain their leaves until late fall. Native Americans have been using willows medicinally for over 2000 years. A mash was made of the bark, which was strapped to the forehead to relieve pain. Its leaves may be made into a tea for treating feverish headaches and arthritis. As with other willows, *Salix irrorata* is popular for making baskets. Other species in the genus *Salix* have been used for wicker furniture. Willow twigs and leaves yield dyes varying from light yellow to greenish gold.

**DESCRIPTION:** **Height** of this deciduous shrub to 4 m (13 ft.); young twigs smooth with a whitish, waxy bloom that can be wiped off; **leaves** alternate, simple, broadly linear to oblanceolate or lanceolate, 5 to 12 cm (2 to 5 in.) in length and 8 to 22 mm (to 1 in.) in width, leaf margins entire or with widely spaced teeth, upper leaf surface dark green and smooth, lower leaf surface lighter green and covered with a waxy coating; **flowers,** female and male borne on separate plants, female flowers are catkins 2.5 to 4 cm (1 to 1.5 in.) long, male flowers are catkins 1.5 to 3 cm (0.5 to 1 in.)

in length, appearing before the leaves; **fruit** a smooth, hairless capsule.

**DISTRIBUTION:** Widespread over most of New Mexico, west to Arizona, north to Colorado.

**HABITAT:** Montane thickets along rivers and creeks and adjacent to intermittent streams at 5,200 to 8,500 ft. (1,600 to 2,600 m) in elevation.

## SAND PENSTEMON
*Penstemon ambiguus*
Snapdragon Family (Scrophulariaceae)

Although there are many penstemons in New Mexico, only a few, including Sand Penstemon, are shrubby. This species is a prolific bloomer, and a handsome addition to a low-elevation native plant garden. It has grass-like leaves and phlox-like, white to pale pink to light purple flowers. Sand Penstemon, as its common name implies, can tolerate sandy soils and has low water requitements. It will grow in full sun, but in very hot areas prefers light shade.

**DESCRIPTION: Height** of this deciduous, many-branched shrub to 60 cm (24 in.); **stems** with tiny fine hairs or smooth, slenderly branched from a woody base; **leaves** opposite, simple, filiform to linear, 1 to 2.5 cm (0.5 to 1 in.) in length, leaf margins entire; **flowers** white at the tip, tubular portion light pink to purple, **fruit** a capsule containing numerous seeds.

**DISTRIBUTION:** Widely scattered throughout New Mexico, west to Arizona, north to Colorado, east to Texas, south to Mexico.

**HABITAT:** Alluvial plains and sandy hills at elevations of 4,000 to 6,000 ft. (1,220 to 1,830 m).

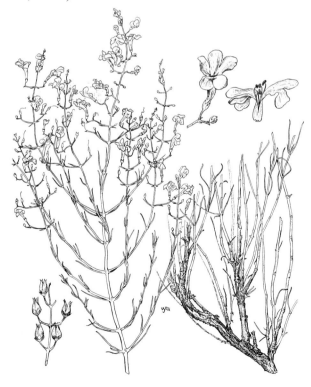

## PALE WOLFBERRY, TOMATILLO
*Lycium pallidum*
Nightshade Family (Solanaceae)

Pale Wolfberry is sometimes an evergreen shrub: with sufficient moisture, it keeps its leaves throughout the winter. Its pale leaves, green, tubular flowers and bright red fruits make it an attractive shrub. Wolfberries are often found around old Indian ruins, because Native Americans gathered and ate the berries, either raw or dried and stored for future use in soups and sauces. During times of famine, they extended the berries with clay, both to make them more filling and to take the bite out of the fruit's bitter taste. Birds and other animals also eat the fruits.

**DESCRIPTION:** **Height** of this shrub to 1 m (3 ft.) or more, with spreading branches; older **stems** reddish-brown, spiny; **leaves** alternate, simple, smooth and hairless, gray-green to blue-green, covered with a whitish coating, fascicled, oblong to spatulate, 1 to 4 cm (0.5 to 1.5 in.) in length, leaf margins entire; **flowers** tubular, greenish-white to greenish-yellow with some purple in the veins, 5-lobed, with stamens extending beyond the petals, flowers borne singly or in pairs; **fruit** a bright red, tomato-shaped berry containing numerous seeds.

**DISTRIBUTION:** Widely scattered over most of New Mexico, west to Arizona, Utah and California, north to Colorado, east to Texas, south to Mexico.

**HABITAT:** Dry hills and plains at elevations of 4,000 to 7,000 ft. (1,220 to 2,130 m).

## CREOSOTE BUSH, HEDIONDILLA
*Larrea tridentata*
Caltrop Family (Zygophyllaceae)

With its glossy, dark green leaves, bright yellow flowers and fuzzy round fruits, Creosote Bush is distinctive and easily recognizable. After it rains, this plant exudes a strong, creosote-like aroma, a characteristic rain-in-the-desert smell that is unlike any other. Although this plant's foliage cannot be tolerated by the majority of insects and mammals, a small desert grasshopper and a walking stick are so closely adapted to Creosote Bush that they eat nothing else. Creosote flowers are visited by about one hundred bee species, some of which are completely dependent upon them for pollen and nectar. Its seeds are eaten by desert animals, and it is used for cover by Gambel and scaled quail. Creosote Bush can be an extremely long-lived species. As the older stems in the middle of the plant die, new stems grow along the edges, becoming essentially a clone of the original plant. One such clone in the Mojave Desert is estimated to be over 11,000 years old. Often called "chaparral" by herbalists, Creosote Bush is used as a salve for skin sores, ringworm and bites, as a tea for stomach and intestinal disorders, and as a poultice for arthritis. Native Americans used the resin from the branches as a glue for pottery and for fixing arrow points.

**DESCRIPTION: Height** of this evergreen shrub to 1.5 m (5 ft.), sometimes reaching 3 m (10 ft.); numerous flexible stems arising from the ground with no well-defined trunk; **leaves** opposite, compound with only 2 leaf-

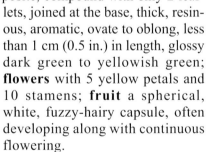

lets, joined at the base, thick, resinous, aromatic, ovate to oblong, less than 1 cm (0.5 in.) in length, glossy dark green to yellowish green; **flowers** with 5 yellow petals and 10 stamens; **fruit** a spherical, white, fuzzy-hairy capsule, often developing along with continuous flowering.

**DISTRIBUTION:** Southwest New Mexico, west to Arizona, Utah, Nevada and California, east to Texas, south to Mexico.

**HABITAT:** Well drained soils and dry mesas at elevations of 3,000 to 5,500 ft. (910 to 1,680 m).

# VINES

Vines can be either woody or herbaceous; here we have included only the woody species. Some vines have tendrils that coil around objects, allowing them to climb. Tendrils can be modified stems, as in ivy or grape, or modified leaves, as in *Clematis*.

To achieve the heights necessary to obtain sunlight, trees invest a lot of energy into growing wood to support their great heights. Vines have evolved a different, and very successful, strategy for obtaining sunlight: they twine around and climb the tall plants (or other suitable objects).

Vines add beauty and grace to your garden. Just give them a trellis, fence, or even a shrub to climb. A honeysuckle or *Clematis* planted outside a window provides beauty, privacy, and relief from the sun all summer long.

"Plants become climbers, in order . . . to reach the light, and to expose a large surface of their leaves to its action. This is effected by climbers with wonderfully little expenditure of organized matter in comparison to trees, which have to support a load of heavy branches by a massive trunk."

Charles Darwin, *The Movements and Habits of*
*Climbing Plants*

## WESTERN WHITE HONEYSUCKLE
*Lonicera albiflora*
Honeysuckle Family (Caprifoliaceae)
**Related Species: Arizona Honeysuckle,** *Lonicera arizonica*

Western White Honeysuckle is an excellent vine for attracting many species of birds to your garden. Humans, too, are captivated by the showy, fragrant flowers and climbing habit of this plant. The specific epithet, *albiflora,* means "white flower." The fruits supposedly contain saponin, a substance sometimes used medicinally to induce vomiting. Some authorities, however, claim that the fruits are fit for human consumption (raw, cooked or dried), although not very tasty.

**DESCRIPTION:** **Length** of this climbing vine to 3 m (10 ft.); **bark** shredding; **leaves** opposite, simple, orbicular to oval, 2.5 to 5 cm (1 to 2 in.) in length, olive green on upper leaf surface, paler below, leaf margins toothless, and hairless; **flowers** white to cream-colored to yellow, funnel-shaped, with two lips and five lobes, five stamens, flowers occurring in clusters at the ends of the branches; **fruit** a round, hairy, few-seeded berry turning black with age.

**DISTRIBUTION:** Southern third of New Mexico, west to Arizona, east to Texas, Oklahoma and Arkansas, south to Mexico.

**HABITAT:** Mountain slopes and canyons at 6,000 to 9,000 ft. (1,830 to 2,740 m) in elevation.

# ARIZONA HONEYSUCKLE
*Lonicera arizonica*
Honeysuckle Family (Caprifoliaceae)
**Related Species: Western White Honeysuckle,** *Lonicera albiflora*
        **Japanese Honeysuckle,** *Lonicera japonica*

Hummingbirds love the nectar in the flowers of Arizona Honeysuckle. Birds and small mammals eat the berries. Arizona Honeysuckle is cultivated because of its fragrant, showy flowers and twining growth habit. Many species of Honeysuckle have been used in making perfumes. Opinions differ on the edibility of *Lonicera* berries: some authorities report that they are edible, but not very tasty. Others claim that they are sometimes used medicinally as a purgative. Another medicinal use of Honeysuckle berries involves making them into a syrup for treating asthma. A close relative of Arizona Honeysuckle, *Lonicera japonica*, Japanese Honeysuckle, is often cultivated. However, it can be an aggressive weed, smothering less vigorous plants. As is so often the case, the native flora is more suitable. Our native Honeysuckles are at least as beautiful as any introduced species.

**DESCRIPTION: Length** of this deciduous climbing vine to 1 m (3 ft.); **bark** shredding; **leaves** opposite, simple, oval to elliptic or oblong, 4 to 7 cm (1.5 to 3 in.) in length, upper leaf surface bluish green, lower surface paler, leaf margins edged with tiny hairs, the upper pair of leaves united at the base, so that the stem appears to pass through the leaf; **flowers** bright

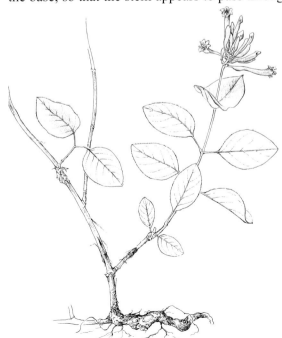

red on the outside and orange on the inside, narrowly funnel-shaped, slightly two-lipped with five petal lobes, flowers in clusters at the ends of the branches; **fruit** a round, red berry.

**DISTRIBUTION:** Western and southcentral New Mexico, west to Arizona and Utah, east to Texas, south to Mexico.

**HABITAT:** Mountains and hill country, open coniferous forests at 6,000 to 9,000 ft. (1,830 to 2,740 m) in elevation.

174

## ROCKY MOUNTAIN CLEMATIS
*Clematis columbiana*
Buttercup Family (Ranunculaceae)
**Synonym:** *Clematis pseudoalpina*
**Related Species: Western Virgin's Bower,** *Clematis ligusticifolia*
                      **Hairy Leatherflower,** *Clematis hirsutissima*

      This attractive vine clambers over shrubs and small trees. In the fall, Rocky Mountain Clematis is distinctive because of its fruits: long, fluffy plumes that are disbursed by the wind. The flowers are large and showy; they do not have true petals, but have petal-like sepals. Rocky Mountain Clematis prefers well-drained soil and does best with its roots in the shade and the rest of the plant in the sun. These vines need a trellis, shrub or a tree trunk to twine around. Rocky Mountain Clematis belongs to Ranunculaceae, the Buttercup family, which is the oldest family of flowering plants. The cut flowers of Clematis are often displayed floating in a bowl.

**DESCRIPTION: Length** of this perennial, trailing or climbing, semi-woody vine to 1.5 m (5 ft.); **leaves** opposite, compound, each leaflet again divided into three leaflets, leaflet margins toothless to toothed to cleft, individual leaflets lanceolate to ovate in shape; **flowers** solitary on leafless stem, thin, drooping, petals absent, sepals light blue to lavender to violet (occasionally white), with numerous stamens, sepals smooth to slightly hairy, be-

coming opaque with age, approximately 3.5 cm (1.5 in.) in length at maturity; **fruit** a round cluster of hairy achenes, appearing as a fuzzy ball.

**DISTRIBUTION:** Western two-thirds of New Mexico, west to Arizona, north to Colorado, South Dakota and Montana.

**HABITAT:** Open to wooded areas and thickets, often found on talus slopes at higher elevations, from 6,000 to 10,000 ft. (1,830 to 3,050 m).

# HAIRY LEATHERFLOWER
*Clematis hirsutissima*
Buttercup Family (Ranunculaceae)
**Synonym:** *Clematis palmeri*
**Related Species: Rocky Mountain Clematis,** *Clematis columbiana*
**Western Virgin's Bower,** *Clematis ligusticifolia*

Hairy Leatherflower is an attractive vine-like shrub for a few reasons: its flowers are deep purple, large and showy; its foliage is unusual and finely divided, and its fruits are long, feathery plumes that are disbursed by the wind. The flowers do not have true petals, but have petal-like sepals. Hairy Leatherflower prefers well-drained soil and does best with its roots in the shade and the rest of the plant in the sun. *Clematis* leaves can be applied to skin sores and made into a wash for infections and scratches. A tea from the dried roots can be used as a diuretic.

**DESCRIPTION: Length** of this climbing or trailing vine or erect shrub, somewhat woody with several stems in a dense clump, 40 to 50 cm (16 to 20 in.); **leaves** densely hairy, opposite, pinnately or bipinnately compound, 7 to 13 leaflets, leaflets deeply lobed or coarsely toothed, leaflets filiform to linear or oblong-lanceolate, averaging 2 to 4.5 cm (0.75 to 1.75 in.) in length and less than 1 cm (0.5 in.) in width; **flowers** one per stem, nodding, bell-shaped, petals absent, sepals four, thick, dark purple with woolly white hairs on outside, 2 to 4.5 cm (0.75 to 1.75 in.) long, curved back at the tips, stamens numerous; **fruit** a round cluster of silvery, hairy achenes, 4 to 6 cm (1.5 to 2.5 in.) long, appearing as a fuzzy ball.

**DISTRIBUTION:** Central New Mexico, west to Arizona, Nevada, Oregon, Montana and Washington, north to Colorado.

**HABITAT:** Foothills and mountains at elevations of 6,000 to 8,000 ft. (1,830 to 2,440 m).

## WESTERN VIRGIN'S BOWER
*Clematis ligusticifolia*
Buttercup Family (Ranunculaceae)
**Synonym:** *Clematis neomexicana*
**Related Species: Drummond's Clematis,** *Clematis drummondii*

Western Virgin's Bower is often found growing over hawthorns, chokecherries, wild plums and other trees and shrubs along stream banks. This is an attractive ornamental, with its clusters of white, star-like flowers and feathery fruits (on female plants only) that persist throughout the winter. The white structures that look like petals are actually petal-like sepals. Western Virgin's Bower is a highly variable species, with differences in the shape and size of the leaflets. It may hybridize with Drummond's Clematis (*Clematis drummondii* ) to form *Clematis neomexicana*. Western Virgin's Bower prefers well-drained soil and does best with its roots in the shade and the rest of the plant in the sun. Several species of birds and small mammals use Western Virgin's Bower for cover, and deer browse the foliage. Native Americans and early settlers chewed this plant as a remedy for sore throats and colds. A wash for infections and scratches for can be made from *Clematis* leaves, and the leaves are applied to skin sores and burns.

**DESCRIPTION: Length** of this climbing vine, somewhat woody near the base, to 6 m (20 ft.); **leaves** opposite, compound, leaflets averaging 3.5 to 8 cm (1.5 to 3.5 in.) in length, smooth or slightly hairy, dark green, leaflets 3 to 7 (usually 5), coarsely toothed or lobed, longer than wide, lanceolate, oblong or ovate, pointed at the tips; **flowers** lacking petals, sepals four to five, petal-like, white, approximately 1 cm (0.5 in.) in length, stamens numerous, male and female flowers borne in clusters on separate plants; **fruit** a dense cluster of achenes, to 5 cm (2 in.) in length, appearing like a fuzzy ball.

**DISTRIBUTION:** Western two-thirds of New Mexico, west to Arizona and California, north to Colorado, North Dakota and Canada.

**HABITAT:** Canyons, stream sides and roadsides at elevations of 4,000 to 8,000 ft. (1,220 to 2,440 m).

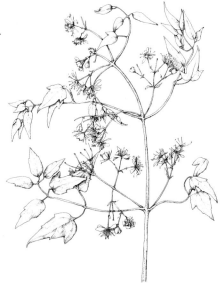

# THICKET CREEPER
*Parthenocissus vitacea*
Grape Family (Vitaceae)
**Synonym:** *Parthenocissus inserta*
**Related Species: Virginia Creeper,** *Parthenocissus quinquefolia*

Thicket Creeper is most often observed climbing trees and walls. It is very handsome with its shiny leaflets and bluish-black berries with red stems, and is especially beautiful in the fall, when its leaves turn bright red. Thicket Creeper is vigorous, rapid-growing, and drought-resistant, and can grow in sun or shade. Its berries are eaten by many species of birds and small mammals, and the foliage provides cover. Thicket Creeper looks beautiful climbing over boulders in a rock garden, up shrubs and trees, or twining up a trellis or fence. It is useful for erosion control on steep banks. The introduced Virginia Creeper is very similar to the native Thicket Creeper. The main differences seem to be that Virginia Creeper's tendrils end in adhesive disks, while Thicket Creeper has few or no disks, the leaflets are thick and dull green in Virginia Creeper but thin and shiny in Thicket Creeper. There is some evidence that the berries of *Parthenocissus* are poisonous to humans, so caution is advised. The leaflets of Thicket Creeper resemble those of Poison Ivy, but Poison Ivy has only three leaflets.

**DESCRIPTION: Length** of this deciduous, climbing or trailing vine to 3 m (10 ft.); woody **stems** reddish brown when young, becoming gray brown with age; tendrils with few if any adhesive disks, branching several times, without flattened tips; **leaves** alternate, palmately compound, leaflets 5 to 7, oblong to lanceolate in shape, thin, 4 to 10 cm (1.5 to 4 in.) in length, leaflet margins coarsely and sharply toothed, upper leaf surface shiny, paler below; **flowers** small, green, inconspicuous, with 5 sepals, 5 petals and 5

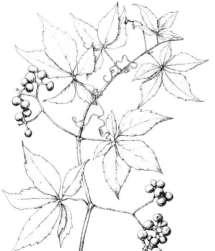

stamens, occurring in flat-topped clusters; **fruit** a round, blue-black berry with red stems, berry thin-fleshed with 1 to 4 seeds.

**DISTRIBUTION:** Common over most of New Mexico, west to Arizona and California, north to Colorado, Wyoming, Montana and Canada, east to western Texas, south to Mexico.

**HABITAT:** Wooded canyons at 4,500 to 7,500 ft. (1,370 to 2,300 m) in elevation.

## CANYON GRAPE
*Vitis arizonica*
Grape Family (Vitaceae)
**Synonyms:** *Vitis treleasei*
*Vitis arizonica* var. *glabra*
**Related Species: Sweet Mountain Grape,** *Vitis monticola*

Canyon Grape belongs to the same genus as table and wine grapes: *Vitis.* Unlike cultivated grapes, though, native southwestern grapes are much easier to grow and require less water. They can grow in very dry air as long as their roots get moisture. Wild grapes can be easily recognized by their climbing habit, generally 3-pointed, serrated leaves, their tendrils, and, in season, their fruits. Old grapevines can be very large, with trunks up to 30 cm in diameter. The genus *Vitis* is very confusing in New Mexico, with authorities disagreeing on differences between species and on how many species occur in the state. Canyon Grape and Sweet Mountain Grape appear to be the most common species. Canyon Grape's fruits make delicious jams and wines, and are readily eaten by many mammals and almost 100 species of birds. Native Americans cultivated Canyon Grape for its fruits and used the leaves and juice for a variety of medicinal remedies.

**DESCRIPTION:** Deciduous, climbing, woody vine; **bark** shredding in long strips; tendrils commonly present; **leaves** alternate, simple, cordate to ovate, gray green on upper surface and hairy on lower surface, often shallowly lobed, palmately veined, up to 18 cm (7 in.) in width, leaves wider than long, leaf margins coarsely toothed, with a deep notch at the base of the leaf; **flowers** small, greenish white, in clusters to 9 cm (3.5 in.) in length, flowers with 5 petals and 5 stamens, flowers both perfect and imperfect on the same plant; **fruits** are blue-black, thin-skinned, juicy berries (grapes), occurring in clusters usually shorter than the leaves.

**DISTRIBUTION:** Southern two-thirds of New Mexico, west to Arizona and Utah, east to Texas, south to Mexico.

**HABITAT:** Ravines and moist areas at elevations of 2,000 to 7,500 ft. (610 to 2,300 m).

# ARBORESCENT CACTI

Cacti have several adaptations that allow them to thrive in arid habitats. Their roots form an extensive mass that spreads out a long way from the plant. The leaves are reduced to spines, protecting the plants from herbivores and reducing the surface area from which the plants lose moisture. Cacti open their stomata (pores on the leaves, or spines) at night, when temperatures are lower and relative humidity is higher, allowing a more efficient use of water.

There are dozens of species of cacti in Arizona and New Mexico. In this book, we have included only the arborescent, or tree-like, species. These cacti are woody, with either flat pads or cylindrical stems.

The pads of some prickly pear species, called *nopalitos*, have traditionally been used for food in the desert Southwest. The fruits of prickly pears and chollas are used for food and wine.

With the exception of some common species, many of our native cacti are threatened by overgrazing and overcollecting. We urge readers to visit these unique plants in their homes, and not bring them to yours.

"The prickly pears across Las Animas County bloom so bright this June -- brilliant masses of waxy yellow and bougainvillea pink against the wet-green vernal prairie -- the whole region has the look of a vast Decoration Day cemetery or borderless, boundless fiesta."

Merrill Gilfillan, *Chokecherry Places,*
*Essays from the High Plains,* 1998

## ENGELMANN PRICKLY PEAR
*Opuntia engelmannii*
Cactus Family (Cactaceae)
**Synonym:** *Opuntia phaeacantha* var. *discata*
**Related Species: Purple-fruited Prickly Pear,** *Opuntia phaeacantha*

Engelmann Prickly Pear is considered to be the largest prickly pear in the Southwest. Its teacup-shaped flowers, lasting just one day, are bright yellow when they open early in the morning, and fade to an apricot color by late afternoon. Prickly Pear pads substitute for leaves in the photosynthetic process. To increase efficiency, the pads are oriented toward the sun during the most active growth time, the summer rainy season. The fruits, known as *tunas* in Spanish, are a staple of Mexican and Native American diets. They are eaten fresh, and can be made into syrups, candies, preserves and wines. The pads, or *nopalitos,* are peeled and the pulp can be eaten fresh, or boiled and then fried or stewed.

Purple-fruited and Engelmann Prickly Pears are quite similar. The main difference seems to be in the spines: in Purple-fruited, one single lower spine is longer than the others in the same areole, and in Engelmann Prickly Pear, the lower spine is the same length as the others in the areole. The genus *Opuntia* can be perplexing, and where the species come in contact with one another, they may hybridize, adding to the confusion.

**DESCRIPTION: Height** of this spiny cactus to 2 m (6.5 ft.); mature **stems** all white or pale gray with age and reddish-brown at the base; **spines** whitish, commonly 1 to 4 per areole, 2.5 to 5 cm (1 to 2 in.) in length, pointing in all directions, lower spine not obviously longer than the others in a single areole; **joints** (pads) broad and flattened, bluish-green, orbicular to elliptic,

20 to 40 cm (8 to 16 in.) in length; **flowers** showy, yellow, borne singly, to 8 cm (3.5 in.) in diameter, petals numerous, sepals petal-like, stamens numerous; **fruit** an obovoid, purple berry, 5 to 8 cm (2 to 3.5 in.) in length.

**DISTRIBUTION:** Southern two-thirds of New Mexico, west to Arizona, east to Texas, south to Mexico.

**HABITAT:** Sandy soils on the plains, arroyos, deserts and grasslands at 3,000 to 5,000 ft. (910 to 1,520 m) in elevation.

## COW'S TONGUE PRICKLY PEAR, TEXAS PRICKLY PEAR
*Opuntia engelmannii* var. *lindheimeri*
Cactus Family (Cactaceae)
**Synonym:** *Opuntia lindheimeri*
**Related Species: Engelmann Prickly Pear,** *Opuntia engelmannii*

The growth habit of Cow's Tongue Prickly Pear tends toward a single trunk, but the plant is usually several angled rather than round as in a tree. To propagate prickly pears, simply expose a pad to the sun for a few days and lay it on the ground; roots will develop from the lower side. Prickly pear fruits, known as *tunas* in Spanish, are eaten fresh, and can be made into syrups, candies, preserves and wines. The pads, or *nopalitos,* are peeled and the pulp can be eaten fresh, or boiled and then fried or stewed. The genus *Opuntia* can be perplexing, and where the species come in contact with one another, they may hybridize, adding to the confusion.

**DESCRIPTION: Height** of this spiny cactus ranges from 1 to 2.5 m (3 to 8 ft.), with a definite cylindrical trunk, erect, or much lower and prostrate; **areoles** with minute glochids, **spines** all yellow or straw colored when young, occasionally red at the base and turning dark gray with age, 1 to 6 spines per areole, spines 1 to 5 cm (0.5 to 2.0 in.) in length, lower spine about the same length as the others in the same areole, spines in all but the lower areoles; **joints** (pads) flattened, obovate or orbicular, green in color, 15 to 30 cm (6 to 12 in.) in length; **flowers** yellow, bowl-shaped, usually one to an areole, 5 to 10 cm (2 to 4 in.) in diameter, petals numerous, sepals petal-like, stamens numerous; **fruit** a purple, obovate to round berry, 3 to 7 cm (1 to 3 in.) in length, with tufts of glochids.

**DISTRIBUTION:** Relatively rare, confined to southern half of New Mexico, east to Texas and Oklahoma, south to Mexico.

**HABITAT:** Grasslands and deserts at elevations of 3,500 to 6,000 ft. (1,070 to 1,830 m).

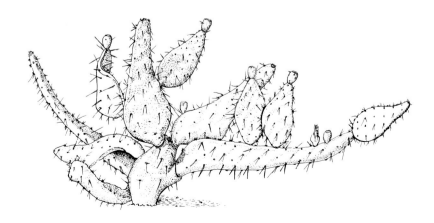

## PURPLE-FRUITED PRICKLY PEAR
*Opuntia phaeacantha*
Cactus Family (Cactaceae)
**Related Species: Engelmann Prickly Pear,** *Opuntia engelmannii*

Purple-fruited Prickly Pear is probably the most widespread and common prickly pear in the Southwest. Although it has a woody base, it doesn't have the form of a tree or shrub. It often grows in a large clump, sprawling along the ground. Prickly Pear pads substitute for leaves in the photosynthetic process. To increase efficiency, the pads are oriented toward the sun during the most active growth time, the summer rainy season. The fruits, also known as *tunas* in Spanish, are eaten fresh, and can be made into syrups, candies, preserves and wines. The pads, or *nopalitos,* are peeled and the pulp can be eaten fresh, or boiled and then fried or stewed. The pulp can also be sun or fire-dried for future use. Bees drink the nectar of Purple-fruited Prickly Pear, in the process acting as pollinators. Javelina, coyote, desert tortoise and other animals eat the fruits. For comparisons between Purple-fruited Prickly Pear and Engelmann Prickly Pear cacti, please see page 180.

**DESCRIPTION: Height** of this spiny cactus, stems mostly prostrate to sprawling, growing in large clumps, to 1 m (3 ft.); mature **spines** brown to brownish-red or dark yellow-red, with the tip often light colored, 2.5 to 8 cm (1 to 3.5 in.) in length, with larger spines flattened at the base, usually 3 or more per areole, with the spines pointing in all directions and with one single lower spine longer than the others; **joints** (pads) flattened, broadly obovate to ovate, 12 to 20 cm (5 to 8 in.) in length; **flowers** showy, yellow, orange or pink, funnel-shaped, borne singly, to 6 cm (2.5 in.) in diameter, numerous petals, sepals petal-like, stamens numerous; **fruit** a wine-colored or dark purple, ovoid berry, 3 to 6 cm (1 to 2.5 in.) in length.

**DISTRIBUTION:** Widespread throughout New Mexico, west to Arizona and Utah, north to Colorado, east to Texas, south to Mexico.

**HABITAT:** Sandy, gravelly and rocky soils, from deserts to grasslands to mountains, at elevations of 3,500 to 7,500 ft. (1,070 to 2,290 m).

# CANDELABRA CHOLLA
*Opuntia imbricata*
Cactus Family **(**Cactaceae**)**
**Synonym:** *Cylindropuntia imbricata*
**Related Species: Cane Cholla,** *Opuntia spinosior*

    Found throughout the Southwest, Candelabra Cholla is the most common tree-like cactus. It is generally seen as a shrub, but in ideal locations can grow into a small tree, with a trunk up to about 25 cm (10 in.) in diameter. Its showy, fuchsia flowers bloom in June and July. New plants sprout readily from joints that fall to the ground. When the plants die, the woody, hollow, cylindrical cores remain. They are used in the creation of unusual art projects, canes, furniture, lamps, etc. Native Americans reportedly ate Candelabra cholla fruits fresh or cooked. Several species of birds (especially the aptly named cactus wren) nest in the spiny branches. Wood (pack) rats use the old, fallen joints to line their nests.

    Candelabra and Cane Chollas look very similar. Probably the easiest way to distinguish them is by their tubercles: Candelabra Cholla's tubercles are long and narrow, while Cane Cholla's tubercles are more rounded.

**DESCRIPTION: Height** of this spiny, woody-stemmed shrubby cactus 1 to 3 m (3 to 10 ft.), often with several branches from the base; **joints** (stems) cylindrical, to 20 cm (8 in.) in length, less than 3 cm (1 in.) in diameter; **tubercles** (swellings from which spines arise) prominent, more than 2 cm (0.75 in.) in length, appearing long and narrow, with 3 or 4 rows usually visible from one side of the stem; **spines** red, pink or brown, normally 10 to 30 per areole, averaging 1 to 2.5 cm (0.5 to 1 in.) or more in length, with numerous smaller glochids arising from areole; **sheaths** on the spines dull tan, persistent throughout the growing season; **flowers** to 7 cm (3 in.) in

diameter, borne at the ends of the stems, petals and petal-like sepals red to pink to purple, stamens numerous; **fruit** a yellow, short (about 3 cm or 1 in.) cylindrical, dry, many-seeded berry, with prominent tubercles and spiny hairs, often persisting throughout winter.

**DISTRIBUTION:** Widespread over New Mexico, west to Arizona and Utah, north to Colorado, east to Texas, Oklahoma and Kansas, south to Mexico.

**HABITAT:** Gravelly and sandy soils, on dry plains and hillsides, at elevations of 3,600 to 6,200 ft. (1,100 to 1,900 m).

## PENCIL CHOLLA, DESERT CHRISTMAS CACTUS
*Opuntia leptocaulis*
Cactus Family **(**Cactaceae)
**Synonym:** *Cylindropuntia leptocaulis*

The specific name, *leptocaulis,* means "slender-stemmed," and this characteristic is indeed one of the easiest ways to identify Pencil Cholla. Look also for the small shrub size, yellowish flowers (about the size of a quarter), and bright red fruits. These fruits, very striking in the winter, are eaten by quail and wild turkeys. The flowers of Pencil Cholla, borne in July and August, open during the hottest part of the day for several days and close at night. Brittle and breaking off at the slightest touch, Pencil Cholla grows easily from fallen joints. It sometimes climbs up the branches of nearby mesquites and other trees and shrubs.

**DESCRIPTION: Height** of this spiny, thicket-forming cactus with woody base, to 1 m (3 ft.); **joints** (stems) round, slender, main branches elongate to 40 cm (16 in.) in length, larger terminal joints green, much shorter than main branches, usually 2.5 to 7.5 cm (1 to 3 in.) long, less than 6 mm (0.25 in.) in diameter, joints smooth or with tubercles only slightly obvious; **areoles** very close together, with very short, white wool, **spines** gray, quite variable in abundance and length, mostly about 2.5 to 5 cm (1 to 2 in.) in length, usually solitary (sometimes 2-3 at an areole), **glochids** few and small; **sheaths** of spines tight or loose, papery, conspicuous, yellow to white or brown; **flowers** 1 to 1.5 cm ( about 0.5 in.) in diameter, petals yellow to green to tan, small and inconspicuous, stamens numerous; **fruit** a red, fleshy, juicy, obovoid to round berry, less than 12 mm (about 0.5 in.) in length, lacking spines but bearing glochids, persisting throughout the winter.

**DISTRIBUTION:** Southern and eastern New Mexico, west to Arizona, east to Texas and Oklahoma, south to Mexico.

**HABITAT:** Mesas, plains and valleys at elevations of 3,000 to 5,000 ft. (910 to 1,520 m).

## AGAVES AND THEIR ALLIES

The flowering plants (angiosperms) are divided into two major classes: Monocotyledoneae and Dicotyledoneae, or monocots and dicots. All the plants in this section belong to the family Agavaceae, and all are monocots.

There are several differences between dicots and monocots, but here we will discuss only the most readily apparent characters. The leaves of monocots have parallel veins, and the leaves of dicots have netted venation. Monocots have flower parts (petals, sepals, and stamens) in 3s or multiples of 3, while dicots' flower parts number 4 or 5.

People often recognize monocots without realizing it. Common monocots in the Southwest are grasses, agaves and yuccas. Monocots include many of our food staples - wheat, rice, corn, etc. - without which humankind would be in trouble. Most monocots - grasses, orchids, lilies, etc. - are herbaceous; the species included in this book are at least somewhat woody.

*"To me there is an appeal to the eternal fitness of things in our native vegetation. It seems at home, a part of the country, and as thoroughly appropriate and in place as an adobe house is in this sun-blest land of ours."*
E. O. Wooton, *Native Ornamental Plants of New Mexico*
New Mexico Agr. Exp. Sta. Bull. 51 (1904)

## PARRY AGAVE
*Agave parryi*
Agave Family (Agavaceae)
**Related Species: Century Plant, Palmer Agave,** *Agave palmeri*

 *Agaves* are some of the most spectacular plants of the southwestern United States. Their large, evergreen, succulent leaves are quite distinctive, but it is their tall flower stalks that really command one's attention. *Agaves* flower just once, usually in eight to twenty years, and then die. But before the parent plant dies, young plants have sprouted from underground runners, ready to take the parent's place in this unusual life cycle. All species of *Agave* are edible, but some are better than others. The caudex (woody base) of the plant is eaten roasted or boiled. Two familiar alcoholic beverages, tequila and mescal, are distillations of fermented *Agave* caudex. The fermented juice yields the intoxicating beverage *pulque*, sometimes described as the national drink of Mexico. A sweet food, also known as mescal, is prepared by removing the leaves and baking the Agave heads in pits lined with hot stones. The Mescalero Apache derived their name from their extensive use of mescal in their diet, and other Native Americans also ate mescal.

 Palmer Agave and Parry Agave are very similar. The leaf shape and size helps to distinguish them: Palmer Agave's leaves are longer and narrower than Parry Agave's.

**DESCRIPTION: Height** of plants with huge, evergreen, succulent leaves forming a basal rosette, often forming colonies from underground sprouts, plants in flower reaching about 4 m (13 ft.); **leaves** succulent, blue-green or gray-green in color, with margins bearing spines curved toward the leaf base, leaf tip ending in a spine, greatly thickened at the base, leaves of mature plants less than 5 times as long as wide, usually 30 to 40 cm (12 to 16 in.) in length and 7 to 10 cm (3 to 4 in.) in width; **flowers** yellow, tinged with red, borne in an open cluster on stalks 3.5 to 4.5 m (12 to 15 ft.) in height, stamens inserted near the top of the floral tube, and extending beyond the flower; **fruit** a capsule to 12 mm (0.5 in.) in length, with flattened black seeds.

**DISTRIBUTION:** Southern New Mexico, west to Arizona, east to Texas, south to Mexico.

**HABITAT:** South-facing, rocky slopes and dry hills at elevations of 4,000 to 6,500 ft. (1,220 to 1,980 m).

# WHEELER SOTOL, DESERT SPOON
*Dasylirion wheeleri*
Agave Family (Agavaceae)
**Related Species: Desert Candle, Smooth Sotol,** *Dasylirion leiophyllum*

Wheeler Sotol flowers throughout the summer months. The female flowers are borne on a separate plant from the male flowers, and are wind-pollinated. Although Sotol's form is similar to Agave, it does not die after flowering. It is sometimes confused with Beargrass, but Sotols' leaves are toothed, much stiffer and less grass-like. Easy to grow from seed, it makes an unusual ornamental. One of its common names, Desert Spoon, comes from the spoon-like depression at the leaf base. Fibers from young leaves can be made into rope. As with *Agave,* the heads of Sotols can be roasted or boiled and the sweet piths and leaf bases eaten by humans. Often, *Agave* and *Sotol* would be roasted together in an open fire pit. The roasted trunks can also be fermented and distilled to yield an intoxicating beverage called

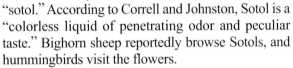

"sotol." According to Correll and Johnston, Sotol is a "colorless liquid of penetrating odor and peculiar taste." Bighorn sheep reportedly browse Sotols, and hummingbirds visit the flowers.

The teeth on their leaves can distinguish Wheeler Sotol and Desert Candle: Wheeler Sotol's teeth point toward the tip of the leaves, and Desert Candle's curve toward the leaf base. Where the two species overlap, they may hybridize.

**DESCRIPTION:** Evergreen plant with a clump of slender, spiny-edged basal leaves arising from a short trunk (trunk often not visible); **leaves** rigid, fibrous, green, somewhat glossy, to almost 1 m (3 ft.) in length, leaves 3 to 4 cm (1 to 1.5 in.) wide, leaf margins bearing teeth that are curved upward or forward, 1.5 to 3 mm long (less than 0.25 in.); **flowers**, male and female, white or greenish, borne on separate plants, in dense narrow clusters on leaf-less stalks up to 4.5 m (15 ft.) in height; **fruit** an obcordate, 3-sided capsule, 7 to 9 mm (less than 0.5 in.) long and 4 to 8 mm (less than 0.5 in.) wide, with 3 papery wings, seeds three angled.

**DISTRIBUTION:** Southern third of New Mexico, west to Arizona, east to Texas, south to Mexico.

**HABITAT:** Rocky or gravelly hillsides at elevations of 3,500 to 6,000 ft. (1,070 to 1,830 m).

## BEARGRASS, SACAHUISTA
*Nolina microcarpa*
Agave Family (Agavaceae)

Although its common name is Beargrass, this plant belongs not to the grass family but to the Agave family. It is related to Agaves, Yuccas and Sotols. Like its relatives, Beargrass is a handsome accent plant in a native garden. Because the growing portion of Beargrass is underground, this species can survive wildfires. The above ground portion of the plant burns and dies, but soon new leaves appear. The inconspicuous flowers of Beargrass are mostly wind-pollinated, but are also visited by bees and wasps. The woody caudex of Beargrass was used as food by Native Americans, who roasted it in open fire pits. The leaf fibers have been used to weave baskets, mats, etc. and are still used for making brooms. The flowers of Beargrass are reported to cause poisoning in sheep and goats.

**DESCRIPTION:** Evergreen shrub with a dense clump of long, narrow leaves at ground level, the woody caudex underground or forming a trunk above ground; **leaves** flexible, grass-like, not spine-tipped, to 1 m (3 ft.) long, 6 to 12 mm (0.25 to 0.5 in.) in width, leaf margins finely serrate and rough to the touch; **flowers** white, less than 1 cm (0.5 in.) in length, numerous in dense clusters, male and female flowers borne on separate plants, flower stalk to 1.5 m (5 ft.) in height, usually not exceeding the leaves; **fruit** a capsule, seeds round.

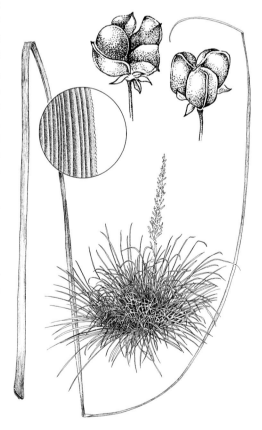

**DISTRIBUTION:** Southern two-thirds of New Mexico, west to Arizona, east to Texas, south to Mexico.

**HABITAT:** Gravelly and sandy soils, on well-drained slopes from woodlands to deserts, at elevations of 3,500 to 7,500 ft. (1,070 to 2,290 m).

## BANANA YUCCA, DATIL YUCCA
*Yucca baccata*
Agave Family (Agavaceae)
**Related Species: Great Plains Yucca,** *Yucca glauca*

The fruit of *Yucca baccata* is banana-like, thus the common name. Native Americans ate the fruits fresh or roasted, or pressed it into cakes and sun-dried them for later use. The seeds and flower buds were also roasted and eaten. For medicinal use, the root is simmered for hours until thick and syrupy, and then applied to sore joints. The saponin in *Yucca* is a steroid derivative, and thus is claimed to be useful in the treatment of arthritis. Banana Yucca can be distinguished from its Yucca relatives by the flower stalk that is (usually) entirely enclosed by the leaves. Unlike other *Yucca* fruits, the fruits of Banana Yucca do not split to disperse their seeds. This task is accomplished by packrats, rabbits and other animals. Banana Yuccas will bloom many times during their lifetimes, but because flowering requires much energy expenditure, they bloom only every few years. Yuccas are important to wildlife: their flowers are eaten by deer, the leaves are eaten by javelina, bighorn sheep, deer and pronghorn, and birds nest in their foliage.

*Yucca baccata* can be distinguished from *Yucca glauca* by the leaf width: the former's leaves are 3 to 5.5 cm (1 to 2 in.) in width, while the latter's leaves are only 1 cm (0.5 in.) wide. Also, the fruits of Banana Yucca are fleshy, plump and as long as 24 cm (9.5 in.), and Great Plains Yucca's fruits are dry and less than 3.5 cm (1.5 in.) in length.

**DESCRIPTION: Height** of this evergreen plant to 1.5 m (5 ft.), with leaves clumped at ground level; **leaves** bluish-green, rigid and dagger-like, broadened toward the middle, commonly straight or curved inward, leaves 30 to 70 cm (12 to 28 in.) in length, 3 to 5.5 cm (1 to 2 in.) wide, leaf margins producing short, coarse, curled fibers; **flowers** waxy, white or cream-colored, sometimes tinged with purple, petals and sepals (3 of each) 6 to 10 cm (2.5 to 4 in.) in length, stamens 6, flowers borne in a cluster on a stalk 35 to 60 cm (14 to 24 in.) in length, entirely within the leaves or only a fraction above them; **fruit** a fleshy, plump, green, cylindrical capsule, to 24 cm (9.5 in.) in length, with many flat, black seeds within.

**DISTRIBUTION:** Widely scattered throughout New Mexico, west to Arizona, Utah, Nevada and California, east to Texas, north to Colorado, south to Mexico.

**HABITAT:** Rocky hill and mountain slopes and plains of grasslands, juniper and oak woodlands at elevations of 3,500 to 7,500 ft. (1,070 to 2,290 m).

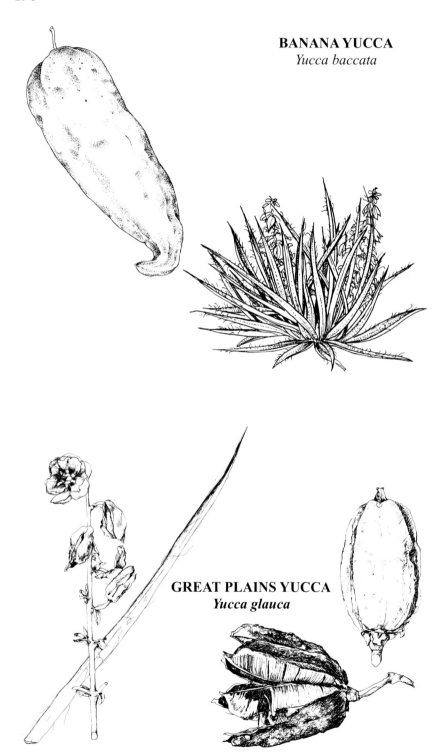

**BANANA YUCCA**
*Yucca baccata*

**GREAT PLAINS YUCCA**
*Yucca glauca*

# GREAT PLAINS YUCCA
*Yucca glauca*
Agave Family (Agavaceae)
**Synonym:** *Yucca angustifolia*
**Related Species: Banana Yucca,** *Yucca baccata*

*Yucca glauca* is the common Yucca of northern New Mexico, extend-ing into the Plains states. Unlike Soaptree Yucca, Great Plains Yucca has no trunk, and grows in a rosette at ground level. This is an excellent species to plant in an area that receives little moisture. *Yucca glauca* has a large root going straight down from each plant, joining onto a large, horizontal storage root, and also many small roots just under the surface. These smaller roots catch moisture from light rains and convey it to the storage root. In this way, Great Plains Yucca can endure many months without rain. Native Americans used a root solution of *Yucca glauca* to kill head lice and stimu-late hair growth. They used the plant for food, too, eating the young flower stalks, flowers and seeds. Great Plains Yucca flowers yield dyes of green, yellow and tan. For comparisons of *Yucca glauca* and *Yucca baccata*, please see pg. 189.

**DESCRIPTION: Height** of this evergreen plant to 1 m (3 ft.) with a short woody stem or stemless, unbranched; **leaves** form a rosette clustered at ground level, gray-green with a narrow white margin from which white threads strip and curl, leaves linear, concave, somewhat flexible, rolled inward at leaf tip, 40 to 60 cm (16 to 23.5 in.) in length, to 1 cm (0.5 in.) wide; **flowers** drooping, to 4 cm (1.5 in.) long, petals three, white, sepals three, greenish white, stamens 5 to 6, flowers borne in a cluster on a leaf-less stalk to 1 m (3 ft.) in height, slightly longer than the leaves; **fruit** a dry, brown, dehiscent, wrinkled, cylindrical capsule, averaging less than 3.5 cm (1.5 in.) in length, with many flat, thin, black seeds within.

**DISTRIBUTION:** Northern two-thirds of New Mexico, north to Colo-rado and Montana, east to the Plains states.

**HABITAT:** Dry, well-drained sandy or limestone soils in open areas, at elevations of 4,000 to 7,500 ft. (1,220 to 2,290 m).

## SOAPTREE, PALMILLA
*Yucca elata*
Agave Family (Agavaceae)

Soaptree is the most widespread of the tree-like Yuccas. Because its form resembles that of palm trees, its Spanish common name is *Palmilla*, or "little palm." *Yucca elata's* roots can be used as shampoos and as washes for linens and wool, earning it another common name, Soaptree. The coarse Yucca fibers were used to weave rope, baskets, sandals and other articles. Native Americans ate the young flower stalks, which resemble great over-grown asparagus. *Yucca elata* sprouts from roots, and may reproduce this way except under the most favorable circumstances, when its seeds germinate. Unlike Agave, which flowers only once, Soaptree will bloom many times in its lifetime, but not every year. *Yuccas* and Yucca moths have a mutualistic relationship: Yucca moths pollinate the yuccas, and lay their eggs at the same time. Upon hatching, the moth larvae feed on some of Yucca's fertile seeds. Yuccas are important to wildlife: their flowers are eaten by deer, the leaves are eaten by javelina, bighorn sheep, deer and pronghorn, and birds, lizards, beetles and spiders nest in their foliage.

**DESCRIPTION: Height** of this evergreen plant to 5 m (17 ft.), tree-like and usually branching, with a woody stem covered with a thick thatch of older dead leaves; **leaves** pale green, flexible, commonly straight, borne in rather symmetrical radiating clusters, leaves 25 to 70 cm (10 to 28 in.) in length, 6 to 12 mm (0.25 to 0.5 in.) wide, leaf margins edged with fine white fibers; **flowers** waxy, white or cream-colored, petals and sepals (3 of each) 3 to 4 cm (1 to 1.5 in.) in length, stamens 6, flowers borne in a cluster on a leafless stalk 1 to 5 m (3 to 17 ft.) in height, greatly exceeding the foliage; **fruit** a dry, green, dehiscent, cylindrical capsule, 4 to 7 cm (1.5 to 3 in.) in length, with many flat, thin, black seeds within.

**DISTRIBUTION:** Central and southern two-thirds of New Mexico, west to Arizona, east to Texas, south to Mexico.

**HABITAT:** Slopes of desert hills, grasslands and dry washes at elevations of 3,500 to 6,000 ft. (1,070 to 1,830 m).

*achene* - a small, dry, indehiscent fruit with a single locule and a single seed attached to the ovary wall at a single point (see Plate V)

*acorn* - a hard, dry fruit of oaks, with a single, large seed and a cup-like base

*acute* - tapering to a pointed apex with more or less straight sides (see Plate III)

*alkaline* - material that is basic rather than acidic, having a pH greater than 7.0

*alternate* - borne singly at each node, as leaves on a stem (compare opposite) (See Plate I)

*anther* - the apical, pollen bearing portion of the stamen (see Palte V)

*apetalous* - without petals

*apex* (pl. *apices*) - the tip; the point farthest from the point of attachment (see Plate III)

*areole* - a small, well-defined area on a surface, as the region of a cactus bearing the flowers and/or spines

*awl-shaped* - short, narrowly triangular, and sharply pointed like an awl (see Plate II)

*axil (or axile)* - the point of the upper angle formed between the axis of a stem and any part (usually a leaf) arising from it (see Plate I)

*axillary* - positioned in or arising in an axil

*axis (*pl. *axes)-* the longitudinal, central supporting structure or line around which various organs are borne, as a stem bearing leaves

*basal* - arising from the base, as leaves arising from the base of the stem

*beak (fruit)* - a narrow or prolonged tip, as on some fruits and seeds

*berry* - a fleshy fruit developing from a single pistil, with several or many seeds, as the tomato (see Plate V)

*bipinnate* - twice pinnate; with the divisions again pinnately divided

*bisexual* - a flower with both male and female reproductive organs (stamens and pistils)

*blade* - the broad part of a leaf or petal (see Plate I)

*bloom* - a whitish, waxy, powdery coating on a surface; the flower

*bristly* - covered with short, stiff, strong hairs

*bud* - an undeveloped shoot or flower (see Plate I)

*calyx* - the outer whorl of modified leaves or sepals at the base of a flower

*capsule* - dry, dehiscent fruit derived from two or more carpels (see Plate V)

*carpel* - a component or highly modified leaf comprising the female reproductive part of a flower

*catkin* - a specialized, scaly, spike-type inflorescence, often pendulous, of apetalous and unisexual flowers as in the birches and willows (see Plate VI)

*caudex* -a short, thickened, often woody base of a perennial plant, usually subterranean or at ground level *cleft* - indentations or incisions cut about half-way to the middle or base

*compound* - composed of two or more like parts; in leaves, with leaf divided into two or more segments (see Plate IV)

*cone* - in gymnosperms, the fruit consisting of a stiff axis and leaf-like scales bearing ovules or pollen

*conical* - cone-shaped, with the point of attachment at the broad end

*conifer* - a cone-bearing plant

*cordate* - heart-shaped, referring to the shape of a leaf or leaf base (see Plate II)

*corolla* - whorl of petals, located above the calyx

*cuneate* - wedge-shaped, triangular and tapering to a point at the base (see Plate III)

*deciduous* - persistent for one growing season; falling off, as leaves that are shed in autumn

*dehiscent (fruit)* - opening at maturity to release contents, as a fruit or an anther

*deltoid* - broadly triangular, length:depth ratio 1:1 (see Plate II)

*dentate* - margins with rounded or sharp, coarse teeth that point outward at right angles to midrib or midvein, teeth cut to one eighth the distance of midrib or midvein (see Plate III)

*disk flower* - a regular flower of the composite or Asteraceae family, as distinquished from the ray flowers in the head (see Plate VI)

*dissected* - deeply divided into many narrow segments

*drupe* - a fleshy, indehiscent fruit with a stony inner fruit wall, as in cherries (see Plate V)

*drupelet* - a small drupe, as in the individual segments of a raspberry fruit

*ellipsoid* - a solid body elliptic in long section and circular in cross section

*elliptic* - a longer than wide shape with the widest axis at the midpoint of the structure and with margins symmetrically curved (see Plate II)

*entire* - without indentations or incisions on margins; smooth (see Plate III)

*evergreen* - bearing green leaves throughout the winter, leaves persistent two or more growing seasons

*fascicle* - cluster or bundle often with commonly attached parts (see Plate IV)

*filiform* - thread-like; filamentous (see Plate II)

*fruit* - a ripened, mature ovary, sometimes including other floral parts which are attached and ripen with it (see Plate V)

*gland* - a protuberance or other structure which secretes sticky or oily substances

*glandular* - bearing glands

*globose* - round, spherical in form

*glochid* - a barbed hair or bristle, as the fine hairs in *Opuntia*

*glossy* - having a smooth, shiny, polished surface

*habitat* - native environment; region where a plant or animal naturally occurs

*head* - a dense inflorescence of flowers on a short or broadened receptacle (see Plate VI)

*herbaceous* - like an herb, not woody; soft and succulent

*husk* - the dry, outer covering of various fruits or seeds, as in an ear of corn

*imperfect* - flowers with either stamens or pistils absent; unisexual flowers

*indehiscent* - not opening at maturity along definite lines or by pores

*inflorescence* - an arrangement or cluster of flowers on the flowering axis (see Plate VI)

*irregular* - bilaterally symmetrical; said of a flower in which all parts are not similar in size and arrangement on the receptacle (compare regular)

*joint* - a section of a stem, as in a pad or segment of a cactus

*lanceolate* - shaped like the head of a lance: elongate with widest point below middle (see Plate II)

*leaflet* - a division of a compound leaf (see Plate I)

*leaf scar* - mark indicating former attachment of a leaf (see Plate I)

*legume* - a usually dry, dehiscent fruit that splits along two sutures, as a pea pod (see Plate V)

*ligulate* - with a ligule

*ligule* - a tongue-shaped, flattened part of the ray corolla common in the Asteraceae

*linear* - long and narrow with parallel margins (see Plate II)

*lobe* - a partial division of a leaf or other structure (see Plate III)

*lobed* - large, round-toothed, cut one-eighth to one-fourth the distance to midvein (see Plate III)

*locule* - cavity or compartment within an ovary or anther (see Plate V)

*lustrous* - glossy, shiny

*margin* - the edge, as in a leaf (see Plate III)

*midrib, midvein* - the central rib or vein of a leaf or other structure (see Plate I)

*montane* - growing in the mountains; the lower vegetation belt on mountains

*net-veined* - with veins forming a network

*node* - region on stem where a leaf, leaves or branches arise (see Plate I)

*nut* - a one-seeded, dry, indehiscent fruit with a hard fruit wall, as in acorns or walnuts (see Plate V)

*nutlet* - a small nut

*obcordate* - inversely cordate, with the attachment at the narrower end; sometimes refers to any leaf with a deeply notched apex

*oblanceolate* - inversely lanceolate; with attachment at narrower end (see Plate II)

*oblong* - elongate with more or less parallel margins (see Plate II) *obovate* - inversely ovate; egg-shaped with the widest point above the middle (see Plate II)

*obovoid* - inversely ovoid, with the attachment at the narrower end

*opposite* - two leaves per node, on opposite sides of stem (see Plate I)

*orbicular* - flat with a circular appearance (see Plate II)

*oval* - broadly elliptic, the width over one-half the length (see Plate II)

*ovary* - expanded basal portion of the pistil that contains the ovules (see Plate V)

*ovate* - egg-shaped: with widest point below middle (compare ovoid) (see Plate II)

*ovoid* - a 3-dimensional, egg-shaped figure with the widest point below middle

*ovule* - embryonic seed; structure that develops into the seed after fertilization (see Plate V)

*palmate* - lobed, veined, or divided from a common point, like the fingers of a hand (see Plate IV)

*panicle* - a branched inflorescence with flowers maturing from the bottom upwards (see Plate VI)

*parallel* - extending in the same direction and at the same distance apart at every point (see Plate I)

*pendulous* - hanging loosely or freely downward

*perfect* - with both stamens and pistils present; bisexual

*persistent* - remaining attached; not falling or shedding

*petal* - a corolla member or segment; a unit of the corolla, usually colored or white (see Plate V)

*petiole* - a leaf stalk (see Plate I)

*pinna* (pl. *pinnae*) - one of the primary divisions or leaflets of a pinnate leaf

*pinnate* - arranged on both sides of a common axis; arranged like a feather (see Plate IV)

*pistil* - the female reproductive part of a flower typically composed of a stigma, style and ovary (see Plate V)

*pith* - centermost tissue or region of a stem or root (see Plate I)

*pod* - the hull or seed case of peas, beans and other legumes

*pollen* - the (usually) yellow powderlike male sex cells on the stamens of a flower

*pollen cone* - a cone bearing pollen: a male cone

*pome* - a berry-like fruit with a bony or leathery inner fruit wall, as in apples (see Plate V)

*prostrate* - lying flat on the ground

*pubescent* - covered with dense or scattered hairs, usually straight and slender

*pyramidal* - a 3-dimensional, short, triangular figure: pyramid-shaped

*raceme* - an unbranched, elongated inflorescence with stalked flowers maturing from the bottom upward (see Plate VI)

*ray flower* - strap-shaped or ligulate flowers, common in head inflorescences of the Asteraceae (see Plate VI)

*receptacle* - the structure which bears and supports the flower parts
(see Plate V)

*recurved* - to curve or bend backward or upward

*reflexed* - directed backward, bent or turned downward

*regular* - radially symmetrical: said of a flower in which all parts are
similar in size and arrangement on the receptacle
(compare irregular)

*resinous* - having a yellowish, sticky exudate or discharge

*reticulate* - netted

*rhizome* - a horizontal underground stem

*riparian* - living on the bank of a stream or river

*rosette* - a circular cluster of leaves, petals or other structures

*samara* - a dry, indehiscent, winged fruit (see Plate V)

*scale* - small, protective non-green leaf on outside of bud; overlapping thin,
flat, flaky or plate-like structures (see Plate IV)

*scaly* - covered with or composed of scales

*seed* - a mature ovule

*seed cone* - a cone bearing seeds; a female cone

*sepal* - a segment of the calyx (see Plate V)

*serrate* - saw-toothed, as along a leaf margin (see Plate III)

*sessile* - attached directly, without a petiole or stalk

*sheath* - portion of an organ which surrounds, at least partly, another organ,
as the leaf base of a grass surrounds the stem

*simple* - undivided; as a leaf blade not separated into leaflets (see Plate I)

*sinus* - space or recess between two lobes or partitions of a leaf

*smooth* - with an even surface; not rough

*solitary* - simple, without others; one flower; not an inflorescence
(see Plate VI)

*spatulate* - like a spatula in shape (see Plate II)

*spike* - an unbranched, elongate inflorescence with sessile flowers
(see Plate VI)

*spine* - a sharp-pointed slender, rigid outgrowth

*stamen* - the male reproductive part of a flower, consisting of an anther and
filament (see Plate V)

*stigma* - the tip of the pistil that receives the pollen, attached directly to the
style (see Plate V)

*strobilus* (pl. strobili) primitive cone-like structure, as in *Ephedra*

*style* - narrowed portion of pistil between the ovary and the stigma
(see Plate V)

*subalpine* - a montane region below timberline

*succulent* - having juicy or pulpy tissues, as in cacti

*tendril* - a long, slender, coiling branch adapted for climbing  (see Plate IV)

*terminal* - at the tip or end of a branch or other structure (see Plate I)

*thorn* - a stiff, woody, modified stem with a sharp point

*timberline* - an imaginary line on mountains above which trees do not grow *trailing* - prostrate and creeping but not rooting

*trifoliate* - a compound leaf with three leaflets (see Plate IV)

*tubercle* - a mound bearing an areole or several spines

*tubular* - cylindrical

*unisexual* - a flower with either male or female reproductive parts,
      but not both

*vine* - weak-stemmed, often climbing plant

*whorl* - a ringlike arrangement of leaves, petals, sepals or other structures:
      a group of three or more leaves or other structures per node
      (see Plate I)

*wing* - thin, flat margin bordering a structure

*woody* - hard and lignified

# ILLUSTRATED GLOSSARY
## Plate I

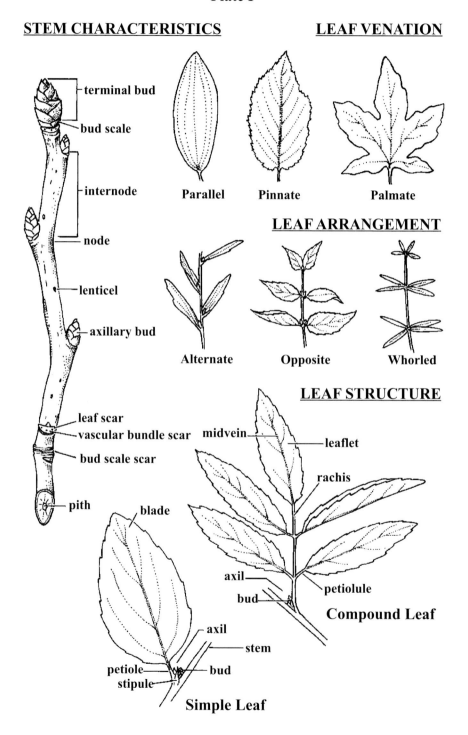

## STEM CHARACTERISTICS

- terminal bud
- bud scale
- internode
- node
- lenticel
- axillary bud
- leaf scar
- vascular bundle scar
- bud scale scar
- pith

## LEAF VENATION

Parallel

Pinnate

Palmate

## LEAF ARRANGEMENT

Alternate

Opposite

Whorled

## LEAF STRUCTURE

- midvein
- leaflet
- rachis
- axil
- bud
- petiolule

**Compound Leaf**

- blade
- axil
- stem
- petiole
- bud
- stipule

**Simple Leaf**

# ILLUSTRATED GLOSSARY
## Plate II

## LEAF SHAPES

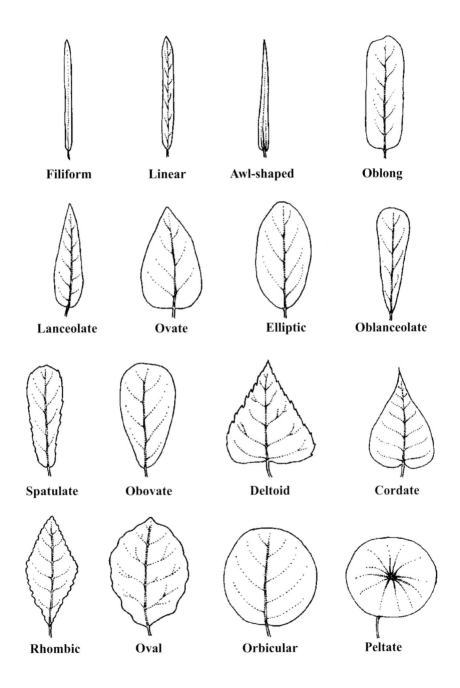

Filiform    Linear    Awl-shaped    Oblong

Lanceolate    Ovate    Elliptic    Oblanceolate

Spatulate    Obovate    Deltoid    Cordate

Rhombic    Oval    Orbicular    Peltate

# ILLUSTRATED GLOSSARY
## PLATE III

## LEAF APICES

Acuminate   Caudate   Acute   Obtuse   Cordate

## LEAF BASES

Attenuate   Cuneate   Obtuse   Rounded   Oblique

## LEAF MARGINS

  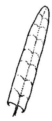 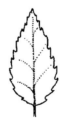  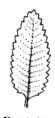

Entire   Undulate   Revolute   Serrate   Biserrate   Dentate

  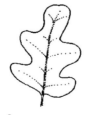  

Crenate   Lobed   Divided   Incised

# ILLUSTRATED GLOSSARY
## PLATE IV

## LEAF MODIFICATION

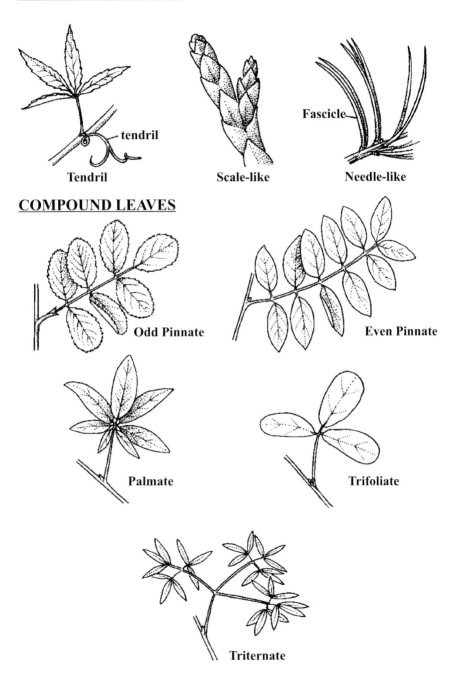

Tendril

tendril

Scale-like

Fascicle

Needle-like

## COMPOUND LEAVES

Odd Pinnate

Even Pinnate

Palmate

Trifoliate

Triternate

# ILLUSTRATED GLOSSARY
## PLATE V

## FLOWER STRUCTURE

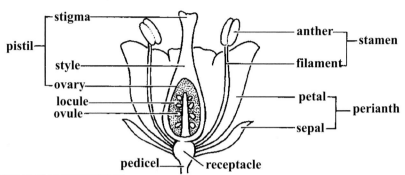

## OVARY POSITION

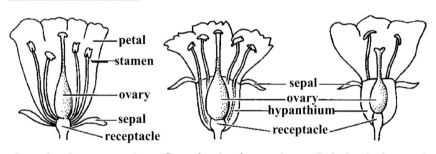

## FRUIT TYPES

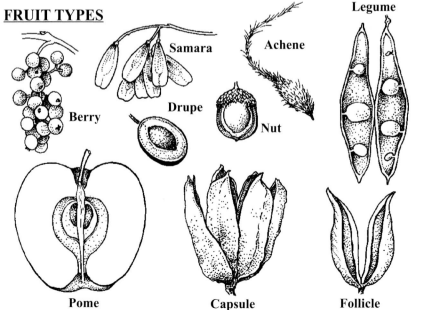

## PLATE VI

### INFLORESCENCES

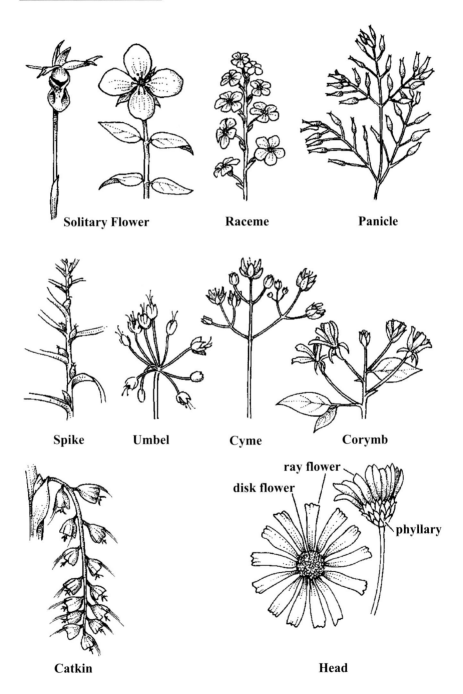

Solitary Flower          Raceme          Panicle

Spike     Umbel     Cyme     Corymb

ray flower
disk flower
phyllary

Catkin          Head

206

# References and Suggested Readings

Allred, Kelly W. 2002. *A Working Index of New Mexico Vascular Plant Names.* Department of Animal and Range Sciences, New Mexico State University.

Beidleman, Linda H., Richard G. Beidleman & Beatrice E. Willard. 2000. *Plants of Rocky Mountain National Park.* Falcon Press.

Benson, Lyman. 1982. *Cacti of the United States and Canada.* Stanford University Press.

Bliss, Anne. 1976. *Rocky Mountain Dye Plants.* Johnson Publishing Co.

Bowers, Janice Emily. 1993. *Shrubs and Trees of the Southwest Deserts.* Southwest Parks and Monuments Association.

Carter, Jack L. 1988. *Trees and Shrubs of Colorado.* Johnson Books.

_____. 1997. *Trees and Shrubs of New Mexico.* Mimbres Publishing Co.

Correll, Donovan Stewart and Marshall Conring Johnston. 1970. *Manual of the Vascular Plants of Texas.* Texas Research Foundation.

Dick-Peddie, William A. 1993. *New Mexico Vegetation: Past, Present and Future.* University of New Mexico Press.

Elmore, Francis H. 1976. *Shrubs and Trees of the Southwest Uplands.* Southwest Parks and Monuments Association.

Epple, Anne Orth. 1995. *A Field Guide to the Plants of Arizona.* Falcon Press.

Flora of North American Editorial Committee, eds. 1993. *Flora of North America North of Mexico.* Vol. 2. Oxford University Press.

Foster, Steven and Varro E. Tyler. 2000. *Tyler's Honest Herbal: A Sensible Guide to the Use of Herbs and Related Remedies.* Haworth Herbal Press.

Foxx, Teralene S. and Dorothy Hoard. 1985. *Flowering Plants of the Southwestern Woodlands.* Otowi Crossing Press.

Grimm, William Carey. 1962. *The Book of Trees.* Hawthorn Books, Inc.

Hardin, James W. and Jay M. Arena, M. D. 1975. *Human Poisoning from Native and Cultivated Plants.* Duke University Press.

Harrar, Ellwood S. and J. George Harrar. 1962. *Guide to Southern Trees.* Dover Publications, Inc.

Harrington, H.D. 1964. *Manual of the Plants of Colorado.* 2 ed. Sage Books.

Heflin, Jean. 1997. *Penstemons: The Beautiful Beardtongues of New Mexico.* Jackrabbit Press.

Ivey, Robert DeWitt. 1995. *Flowering Plants of New Mexico.* Published by the Author.

Kartesz, John T. 1994. *A Synonymized Checklist of the Vascular Flora of the United States, Canada, and Greenland.* Vol. I - II. Timber Press.

Kearney, Thomas H. & Robert H. Peebles. 1951. *Arizona Flora.* University of California Press.

Kelly, George W. 1970. *A Guide to the Woody Plants of Colorado.* Pruett Publishing Co.

Kingsbury, John M. 1964. *Poisonous Plants of the United States and Canada.* Prentice-Hall.

Kirk, Donald. 1970. *Wild Edible Plants of the Western United States.* Naturegraph Publishers.

Lamb, Samuel H. 1989. *Woody Plants of the Southwest.* Sunstone Press.

Lewington, Anna. 1990. *Plants for People.* Oxford University Press.

Lewis, Walter H. and Memory P. F. Elvin-Lewis. 1977. *Medical Botany: Plants Affecting Man's Health.* John Wiley and Sons.

Little, Elbert L., Jr. 1950. *Southwestern Trees: A Guide to the Native Species of New Mexico and Arizona.* USDA Forest Service, Agriculture Handbook No. 9.

Martin, W.C. & C.R. Hutchins. 1980. *A Flora of New Mexico.* Vol. I-II. A.R.Gantner Verlag K.G. (J. Cramer).

_____. 1984. *Spring Wildflowers of New Mexico.* University of New Mexico Press.

_____. 1986. *Summer Wildflowers of New Mexico.* University of New Mexico Press.

_____. 1988. *Fall Wildflowers of New Mexico.* University of New Mexico Press.

Moore, Michael. 1992. *Los Remedios: Traditional Herbal Remedies of the Southwest.* Red Crane Books.

Moore, Randy, W. Dennis Clark and Kingsley R. Stern. 1995. *Botany.* Wm. C. Brown Co.

Peattie, Donald Culross. 1991. *A Natural History of Western Trees.* Houghton Mifflin.

Perry, Jesse P. Jr. 1991. *The Pines of Mexico and Central America.* Timber Press.

Powell, A. Michael. 1988. *Trees and Shrubs of Trans-Pecos Texas.* Big Bend Natural History Association, Inc.

Radford, Albert E. 1986. *Fundamentals of Plant Systematics.* Harper and Row.

Simpson, Benny J. 1988. *Texas Monthly Field Guide Series: A Field Guide to Texas Trees.* Gulf Publishing Company.

Stephens, H.A. 1973. *Woody Plants of the North Central Plains.* The University Press of Kansas.

Thomas, Peter. 2000. *Trees: Their Natural History.* Cambridge University Press.

Vines, Robert A. 1960. *Trees, Shrubs and Woody Vines of the Southwest.* University of Texas Press.

Wasowski, Sally and Andy Wasowski. 1995. *Native Gardens for Dry Climates.* Clarkson, Potter Publishers.

Weber, William A. 1990. *Colorado Flora: Eastern Slope.* University Press of Colorado.

_____. 1996. *Colorado Flora: Western Slope.* University Press of Colorado.

Welsh, Stanley L., N. Duane Atwood, Sherel Goodrich & Larry C. Higgins (Editors). 1987. *A Utah Flora.* Great Basin Naturalist Memoirs, Number 9, Brigham Young University.

Photographs are referred to in **boldface** type

**P**

*Portulaca suffrutescens*  **70**
*Prosopis glandulosa*  **41**, 141
*Prunus serotina*  **28**, 115
*Prunus virginiana*  **28**, 115
*Pseudotsuga menziesii* var.
              *glauca* **16**, 75, 88
*Psorothamnus scoparius*  **40**, 142
*Ptelea trifoliata*  **29**, 116
*Purshia stansburiana*  **50**, 163

**Q**

*Quercus emoryi*  **27**, 111, 113
*Quercus gambelii*  **26**, 112
*Quercus grisea*  **27**, 113
*Quercus hypoleucoides*  **42**, 144

**R**

*Rafinesquia neomexicana*  **64**
*Ratibida columnifera*  **64**
*Rhus glabra*  **32**, 122
*Rhus trilobata* **31**, 121
*Ribes aureum*  **43**, 146
*Ribes cereum*  **43**, 147
*Ribes pinetorum*  **43**, 148
*Ribes wolfii*  **43**, 149
*Robinia neomexicana*  **26**, 110
*Rosa woodsii*  **51**, 164
*Rubus parviflorus*  **51**, 165

**S**

*Salix exigua*  **52**, 166
*Salix gooddingii*  **20**, 100
*Salix irrorata*  **52**, 167
*Salvia pinguifolia*  **45**, 152
*Sambucus cerulea*  **24**,  107
*Sambucus racemosa*
          var. *microbotrys* **25**, 108
*Sapindus saponaria*  **21**, 101
*Senecio flaccidus* var. *douglasii*
                  **35**, 129
*Silene laciniata*  **66**

**S**

*Sophora secundiflora*  **41**, 143
*Sphaeralcea ambigua*  **67**
*Symphoricarpos rotundifolius*
**T**                          **37**, 132

*Toxicodendron rydbergii* 93

**V**

*Vitis arizonica*  **55**,  178
*Vitis monticola* 178

**Y**

*Yucca baccata*  **60**, 185, 189-190
*Yucca elata*  **61**, 192
*Yucca glauca* **61**, 190-191

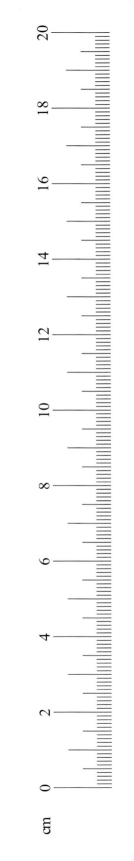